dream rooms

Andreas von Einsiedel

Johanna Thornycroft

dream rooms

inspirational interiors from 100 homes

MERRELL

LONDON · NEW YORK

Today's dream rooms, with some exceptions, are a celebration of predominantly neutral, calming and comfortable environments, very much confirming that owners and designers treat the design, decoration and colouring of home interiors as an antidote to the speed and pressure of modern living. Clutter, bright colours and masses of furniture can be chaotic and distracting. In our earlier books, *Dream Homes* (2005) and *More Dream Homes* (2008), there was a little more colour and pattern than appear here, although neutral and white interiors were beginning to make their mark internationally.

Garden rooms, courtyards, terraces and pools also feature much more pared-down design and landscaping, with the planting often limited to myriad tones of green with white, while limestone of various types is the most popular material for steps, edging and hard surfaces. Timber-decked patios and terraces, once nearly always varnished (and rather too orange), are left to weather naturally, producing the lovely silver-grey hues of bleached wood.

White was always the preferred choice of Modernists, but all-white or toned-white interior schemes have become the norm in a multitude of architectural styles. In older houses, the whites tend not to be brilliant, and incline instead towards soft-grey, soft-green, stone and mouse tones. Solid blocks of strong colour and elaborate printed curtain designs, along with floral wallpaper, are now found almost exclusively in period country houses, and remain as charming as ever. Where pattern is chosen, it is most likely to be a single wall of perhaps an over-scaled, newly coloured paper, Cole & Son having set the benchmark for the reinterpretation of historic designs; this was succeeded by talented young designers who favour over-scaled, organic or naturalistic forms. Geometric patterns in the style of David Hicks (1929–1998) are making a comeback at the design shows, along with beautifully coloured, ikat-inspired designs.

Wooden floorboards, ranging from almost black to almost white, are still the most popular flooring material for every room. Wood feels soft and warm, compared to the hard, cool feel of stone or tile, and many boards are suitable for underfloor heating. Sisal and seagrass, once used in a wall-to-wall treatment, are now more commonly cut into rug sizes edged with linen tape. Rug designers have created startling new designs in wonderful colours, and stripes remain a classic choice. Fine Persian and other oriental rugs have not disappeared altogether, but remain the choice of country-house owners rather than young, urban apartment dwellers. Bold, graphic nomadic rugs and chequerboard or antique kilims are favoured, rather than the traditional, and very expensive, silk floral carpets made in the great centres of Isfahan, Tabriz and elsewhere. Many people do not bother with carpets or rugs at all, or use them perhaps only in bedrooms. Even in chilly northern Europe, carpets and rugs are no longer deemed essential for warmth.

Greater attention is being paid to – and ever-larger slices of budgets are invested in – kitchens,

bathrooms and the inclusion of work areas. The large one-bedroom apartment used to be a rarity, but the rising number of single people or couples who choose to have no children means that space is being configured on a much more individual basis. Until fairly recently, the number of bedrooms in an apartment or house, rather than the total square footage of available living-space, was a key consideration when buying a property. Nowadays those extra bedrooms are most likely to be carefully considered for their suitability for conversion into a luxury en-suite bathroom, a home office or an extension of some other living-area. Even in large homes, there is a reluctance to set aside rooms for such specific single purposes as dining or cooking: it is more sociable to combine the two functions, and we gravitate to the kitchen as never before. Eat-in kitchens are nothing new, but owners and designers now treat these dual or multiple functions in a fresh, more cohesive and exciting decorative way, planning and integrating the space as a whole.

The home-working trend is set to continue. As a result of communications development, travel congestion and cost, many people work at home for at least some of the time. Where no separate space can be allocated to an office, designers and manufacturers of storage systems, desks and chairs have risen to the challenge of providing functional and efficient ways to work, often in ever-smaller spaces. As wireless communications have emerged, a traditional desk has become less important, although, by and large, the much-heralded 'paperless' world has yet to arrive. We print as many documents as ever, so for the foreseeable future, a home office in some guise will continue to be an essential part of our domestic lives.

Interior fashion moves apace. Its velocity may slow somewhat during recessionary times, partly because people move less frequently, but new fabric and carpet collections continue to be launched, along with ranges of furniture and lighting, bathroom fittings and kitchens, floor tiles and door handles. The process of innovation and fresh design, adopting new materials and subtle changes in fashionable colouring, remains unstoppable – and rightly so.

What is very clear is the continued passion for twentieth-century design items, from 1930s and 1940s bathroom fittings to all manner of furniture, lighting, glassware and art. The young London designer Rui Ribeiro has collected furniture by the likes of Bruce James Talbert, Ambrose Heal, Christopher Dresser and Gordon Russell for his 1930s Tudor-revival home (no. 20: see p. 332). By mixing up these pieces with his own designs, along with modern art, ceramics and photography, he has created thoroughly contemporary, eclectic interiors. He believes, and many would agree with him, that 'interiors need three distinct elements – found items, custom-designed pieces and antiques'.

There are, however, several homes illustrated in *Dream Rooms* where time appears to have stood still: for example, a wonderful castle in Ireland (no. 22, Ballinlough: see p. 333) and a thoroughly traditional home in Provence (no. 52: see p. 339). It would be a sad day if traditional decoration and furnishings – antique or modern pieces made and bought locally – such as are abundantly deployed in these homes, were to disappear for ever. Equally, the three-year restoration of an early Lutyens house (no. 3: see p. 328) by the leading London architectural designer John Minshaw illustrates how a run-down, important period home can be brought up to date in an exemplary manner. Here, old fuses with new, both structurally as well as by mixing fine antique furniture with custom-designed pieces, and – as Lutyens preferred during his career – using the finest English materials.

In this book we show contemporary homes by the Mexican father-and-son team Legorreta and Legorreta (no. 49: see p. 339), Studio Matteo Thun in Milan (no. 34: see p. 336), and stunning work by Bruno and Alexandre Lafourcade in Provence (nos. 1, 18, 30, 40, 52 and 81: see pp. 328, 332, 335, 337, 339 and 345). Probably the most unusual modern design is that of Jean-François Zevaco for a client near Marrakesh (no. 15: see p. 331). Sometimes an architect has a major influence on interior decoration and the choice and supply of all the furniture (illustrated here by the Matteo Thun house, no. 34), as was common in the eighteenth century. What is always fascinating in such a compilation of interiors as *Dream Rooms* is the talent that non-professional owners display. Some may be less rigorous, but they never lack character and a sense of celebration of individual style; significantly, most of the owners whose homes appear here –

whether stylists or photographers, writers or fabric designers – seem to work in a creative environment. Good interior design and decoration are not for the faint-hearted complete amateur.

As with everything to do with home life, comfort and security are the primary factors in the making of dream rooms, but indulgence plays a part as well. The decoration and contents of one's most personal space are highly individual matters, not, of course, based on entirely practical needs. The creation of a great interior can indeed be a labour of love, where a home evolves slowly, rather than 'being done' in one go. It may involve waiting for that all-important chair or picture to come up at auction, to satisfy the desire for original twentieth-century pieces rather than reproductions; or patiently saving to afford the conversion of a bedroom into a dream dressing-room, custom-fitted to store every handbag and pair of shoes, and all of one's clothes, in a perfectly ordered space.

Rather than anatomizing whole houses, *Dream Rooms* provides a journey through a myriad of rooms, grouped according to their function. We focus on various styles and the elements that conspire to create them. The idea is to provide inspiration, foster new ideas and remind readers that classic contemporary design, in particular, endures. We hope professionals and amateurs alike will find much to excite their creative imaginations and will revel in the wealth of quality workmanship and beauty that are revealed in these pages.

Living

In many ways, living-rooms remain as they were in the days when they were considered the 'best' room (usually the front or drawing-room) – a showcase for taste, confidence and wealth, and, to some extent, a place in which to vaunt one's knowledge of and admiration for modernity. In times gone by, guests were carefully steered to the front room, and gained little idea of the rest of the accommodation. It is still true that, apart from the multi-purpose living-space – which is a hard-working but more social and less formal combination of cooking, dining and living – modern living-rooms, whether opulent, contemporary or austere, tend to be reserved for more formal use.

Symmetry plays an important role in the design of living-rooms, especially where a fireplace is a focal point. Human nature appears to prefer order and rationality, at least on the surface. Many of the rooms illustrated can be described as classic – beyond fashion, although they contain fashionable pieces, combined with more traditional ones. It is also interesting to look back a few years to a time when design commentators noted that the mid-twentieth-century desire for open-plan Modernism had waned. In the early 1980s the return to traditional comforts, aesthetics and nostalgia – English country-house style being the clear leader – was in the ascendancy. Things move on. While the kitchen may now be the real heart of a home (pages 117–151), the exhilarating variety of styles displayed in modern living-rooms indicates a continuing passion for highlighting beauty, taste and one's favourite objects in what is, most likely, the largest room in a home.

Contemporary

A contemporary interior is primarily distinguished by the size and shape of the seating that furnishes it. Our way of life has changed from sitting upright – on hard little sofas and chairs – to lounging and relaxing on long, broad, down-filled sofas that are large enough to sleep on, and seating, whether vintage or the latest design, is often boxy in shape. Window treatments, fireplaces and the choice of colour are also important factors in this look: all tend to be pared down to the simplest of elements.

Architecture, too, can play a role: modern houses with glass walls are rarely decorated and furnished in a strictly traditional sense, but the tremendous popularity of vintage design pieces continues to feature in contemporary style. Everything is low, including side and coffee tables and chair seats. The floor itself can be an important living-space: contemporary design allows a room to breathe, so empty space is not a taboo.

Contemporary

These rooms reveal a few more key features of contemporary style. Maximum use of all the available light provides a strong contemporary feel: curtains – where there are any – are barely visible and not treated as an important part of the design. In many ways the image top, right, appears to show the most contemporary living-room here, but the building, including this top-floor apartment, was in fact designed and

built by Berthold Lubetkin in the 1930s. The owner managed to purchase some of the original furniture, including the two cowhide chairs seen here, which were also designed by the architect for this, his own apartment.

Within a Victorian house, opposite, a London interior designer stripped out a double-volume space with a mansard roof to create a greatly simplified living-room. The Minotti L-shaped seating, fired-acacia floors and Deirdre Dyson rug are all 'of the moment'.

Contemporary

While monochrome or neutral colour schemes continue to be the choice of many (see pages 30–31), others like a 'shot' of primary or bright colour to accessorize or bring an accent to a room. A sunken seating area in a modern Marrakesh house (opposite, top) could have been dominated by the floors and massive wooden sculpture placed on the upper level, but a huge painting and the Prussian-blue *tadelakt* wall 'lift' the honey-coloured timber.

Red and orange are a cheerful, youthful and fun combination. Three *Panto Pops* floor seats are perfect for the children who live in a penthouse conversion in south London (opposite, bottom centre); red upholstery and an orange 'ashtray' coffee table also enliven an otherwise all-white living-room on the French south coast (opposite, bottom right). Orange was again chosen to set off an enormous mirror above the fireplace in a house near Marbella (below); the designer also chose orange tones for the curtains, cushions and pictures.

Traditional

When applied to the living-room, 'traditional' always used to mean elaborate curtain treatments; tabletops crammed with collections of all sorts of things; oriental rugs; a lot of furniture upholstered in multicoloured prints; and papered or 'paint-effect' walls, likewise crammed with pictures, sconces and mirrors. But much modern traditional style has a strongly Georgian feel about it, featuring bare floorboards, uncluttered windows, space, and a lightness that disappeared in the late twentieth century.

Opposite, bottom, the panelled room in a London Arts and Crafts house contains some fine furniture of the same period: it is traditional in scope but modern in the arrangement of the pieces. As we saw earlier (pages 14–15), sofas and chairs are now much larger than before, but the choice of 'button' upholstery on an ottoman stool, an original Purbeck marble fireplace and fine period portraits (right) evokes a strong sense of tradition. Antiques alone do not create a traditional interior; nonetheless, a carefully selected mix of old and new, patina and architectural details can all be blended to produce a comforting feeling of tradition.

Traditional

All but one of the mellow, unpretentious and welcoming rooms shown here are country living-rooms in, variously, Ireland, England and France. A hall is also included, as many are used as additional living-spaces rather than simply as a transition from one room to another.

Each house is partly or wholly of eighteenth-century construction, and each of these living-rooms is decorated and furnished to provide a sense of well-being and comfort, peace and repose, where fine old fireplaces, along with heirloom antiques and objects bought for pleasure, enhance the period atmosphere. Such rooms as these suit colourful fresh flowers and potted plants, table lamps and silk shades, mismatched furniture and small tables that can be moved about as required. While traditional living-rooms appear formal, they are flexible spaces, capable of accommodating large parties or providing a welcome haven away from the kitchen or work.

Tall Lights

It is a vexing fact that, almost from the moment the light bulb was invented, designers produced an extraordinary range of public street-lighting designs, table lamps, wall lamps and pendant fittings, but very few floor lamps. For decades the standard was a wooden column with a wobbly, tasselled shade on top. Yet floor lights or very tall table lamps can contribute far more to a room than simply lighting a shelf or a dark corner. Their shapes – frequently sculptural, colourful, weird and wonderful – add life and interest to an interior. Far left is an elegant design by Marc Newson; left, Jean-Louis Domecq offers a free-standing and vibrant version of the angle-poise; while below, left is a thoroughly original, striking light by Cattelani & Smith. As ever, the specific choice of the light says a lot about the person who chooses it: usually young, with quirky taste and possessions, and a firm belief in eclecticism. In Marrakesh, for example (opposite), the snake-like shape of this lamp is intriguing; it is possibly a prototype, as the designer is unknown.

Since so many of the designs available tend to the idiosyncratic, tall lighting does not easily work in such traditional interiors as a country house furnished with antiques and chintz fabrics: the divergence of styles is too great. But if your taste is adventurous, Italian designers in particular continue to push the boundaries in contemporary lighting design: there is now an enormous and always exciting selection on offer.

Side Lights

With a little ingenuity, side lights can provide discreet and surprisingly flexible solutions to the problem of lighting a living-room effectively. For example, by fixing a pair of vintage metal lights directly on to the oak-clad wall of this large room in a French chateau (right), the designer immediately managed to illuminate the large bench area without introducing further tables or floor lamps that would clutter the streamlined space. The other considerable benefit of this design is that the fittings can be swung in a half-circle, or directed up or down. In another part of the same living-room (below), a circular glass lamp base and its shade are positioned on a round table, creating a good mix of curves with straight lines (entirely linear design is rarely exciting).

As lighting technology moves on, the use of modern materials produces some surprising designs and dramatic effects. Note how the white lampshade (far right), at first seeming to float on its own, rests lightly in its red upright support. The Italian designer of the modern Spanish house opposite chose the furnishings and lighting almost exclusively from Italian suppliers. The smooth, glossy side-table lights, in pure white, came from Flos Spa in Brescia.

Alternative Lighting Solutions

Through the decades since electric lighting was developed, designers have produced an astonishing array of lighting creations. An Arts and Crafts building, converted into a modern London home (opposite, top right), features three original *Artichoke* lights, possibly the most beautiful pendant lights ever designed. Poul Henningsen designed the PH *Artichoke* light in 1957. Available in brushed copper, stainless steel or enamel, its fragmented, overlapping flaps produce a dazzling effect.

The wonderful Viennese bronze light, still with its original silk-and-linen panels (opposite, bottom right), belongs to a London couturier. The elegant and original soldered-pipe lamp bases on either side of the sofa in a converted warehouse in London (opposite, left) are the work of the apartment's owner, a designer of metal lighting and dazzling chandeliers.

One of the great qualities of smaller lamps (below) is their versatility. The plainest little lamp base can be dressed up with many styles of shade, from bright floral cotton to refined pleated silks.

Neutrals

Neutral decoration can range from a pure-white scheme where the room itself and everything in it are a single tone, to many layers and variations of closely related colours. In estate agents' language, 'neutrals' used to mean bland, unexciting and downright dull, consisting of tinted-white paintwork, verging on pink or yellow, and with matching carpets. Today's use of neutral colour schemes is altogether more sophisticated, subtle and

much better planned, taking into account how texture adds a dimension even where colours may be entirely matching, and the way in which both daylight and modern lighting affect interiors.

There is something of an ethereal beauty about the palest of rooms and furnishings. Perhaps the effect is heightened by the sheer luxury of appearing not to have to worry about scuffs or stains, pollution or grime; or it may be that such schemes remind us of the tropics and holidays. Certainly, in the

early 1990s all good paint suppliers took notice when the demand for 'soft' whites took hold; brilliant white, which has a hint of blue, would never have worked in the beautifully crafted rooms seen here. Instead, designers have developed their favourite palette of whites according to the architecture, light source and flooring in their clients' homes, working in a range of cool to warm tints.

Contrasting Colours

One of the great classic colour combinations is blue and brown. Below is a perfect example of duck- or bird's-egg blue-green paint and a curved sofa upholstered in fabric of a similar tone, teamed with rich-brown detailing, skilfully used on the ceiling; as neat finishing panels to the walls either side of the curved glass doors; on the floors; and in the rug. The colour of iron or bronze is also a perfect neutral; whether grey, green or nearly black, the tones change according to the light.

Dark mahogany brown enhances the feeling of depth, so well illustrated – opposite, bottom right – where a shallow alcove appears deeper than it is really is, with the antique oval-topped pier-glass mirrors reflecting light and giving the room an impressive sense of drama and scale. Against this background, the exceptionally deep Howard chairs and wide sofa are thrown into dramatic relief. In a more homely but nonetheless effective style (opposite, top right), an antique wooden chair, the stripe in a rug, and an old basket all provide natural hues in the myriad tones of brown that constitute such a decorating classic.

Pastel Colours

By the early eighteenth century, the fact that it was possible to manufacture new, lighter paint colours was having a profound effect upon interior decoration. The Rococo period had begun, driven by Madame de Pompadour, who influenced design all over Europe. Colours named 'Palace Cream', 'Powder Pink', 'Cloud White' and 'Apple Green' must have been a revelation after the tradition of drabs, greys, earth browns and greens.

Pastels have never entirely gone out of fashion, especially in bedrooms, and a palette of pinks, creams and greens, pale blues and lilacs adds depth and warmth to living-rooms. The starting-point might be a rug, a piece of fabric or a painting; the picture above the sofa (right), set against a background colour of light blue, is certainly comprised of a lovely mix of inspiring colours. Even where the walls are white (below), pastel linen upholstery, in solid blocks of colour, enlivens an otherwise neutral scheme, giving the room a more individual and personal flavour.

Blues and Purples

Blue, on walls, can be a notoriously cool colour, and is often used only in small, dark rooms. It works extremely well, however, when broken up by mirrors and pictures, and is greatly complemented by orange and red. The use of blue lighting at cornice and floor level creates both drama and atmosphere in a London living-room (opposite). This is a very carefully thought-out interior finish, in which texture, shadow and colour play important roles.

The choice of 'warm' blue creates a sense of 'night sky' that is mysterious and rather magical. In his own house (left), a German designer favours deep-toned walls, which show as a potent indigo where daylight penetrates, and change to inky, muted blue in the shadows. The smaller sitting-room-cum-library (below) is painted in lilac tones, an unusual colour for overall decorating; but with the lilac balanced here by the strong shapes and dark colours of the bookshelves, lampshades, chest and table, the room becomes an intimate and luxurious bolthole.

Reds and Oranges

Whether in town or the country, and in ancient or modern architecture, red and orange are stimulating colours, warm and friendly in any climate. The brown-toned reds used in this magnificent eighteenth-century first-floor drawing-room (right) set off the fine fire surround, gilt picture-frames and antique furniture to perfection. In Normandy (below) coral red was the choice of the owner–designer for his en-suite sitting-room, where most of the period panelling had survived for more than two hundred years. The most traditional colours of Provence range from deep muted red to the almost apricot colour shown opposite, bottom right: here, a fine collection of honey-toned regional furniture and art blends in a calm composition.

As we have seen (pages 18–19), red and orange are also most effective as highlight or accent colours. In a modern house in Spain (opposite, top left), orange paint and fabric and a picture containing an orange stripe add vibrancy to an otherwise all-white setting. Likewise, in a London apartment (opposite, top right), an old chair is upholstered in red suede, the lampshade is made of red-and-gold velvet, and the red-and-green silk *lawon* on the wall adds yet another tonal variation.

Yellows and Golds

Yellow makes us smile; its effect is sunny, upbeat and positive, whether in warm or cool tones, ranging from acid to egg-yolk, daffodil to cream and gold. In London, at least two famous yellow rooms are greatly admired by the decorating fraternity worldwide: the drawing-room at the Sir John Soane's Museum in Lincoln's Inn Fields, and Nancy Lancaster's 'butter-yellow' drawing-room at Avery Row in Mayfair. Sadly, such exuberant decoration has largely gone out of fashion, although the intense yellow walls of the living-room shown opposite, top left, at least mimic Soane's chrome-yellow masterpiece.

Yellow and grey were always a great combination: a modern mix of gold and grey silk velvet against gold-glazed walls in a Spanish guest house (below) looks subtly fresh and smart. The decoration of a late seventeenth-century London house (opposite, bottom right) has a Regency feel to it, partly achieved by the use of yellow silk curtains and linen chair covers. Period furniture, strong black accents and the way the furniture is laid out all combine to produce a modern but classic scheme.

Contemporary Fireplaces

The 'hole-in-the-wall' fireplace, lacking any sort of decoration and pared down to a box-like form, signalled a change in the treatment of fireplaces where no significant change (other than, in the twentieth century, the arrival of the electric-bar heater fitted into the space) had taken place for hundreds of years. Urban fireplaces now contain almost exclusively gas flames and are largely decorative, providing a comforting amount of light rather than a primary heat source. Opposite, the typically very narrow rooms in Moroccan riads can be difficult to furnish, but here the owner cleverly made the fireplace almost as wide as the room, thereby increasing the sense of space. By placing a small sofa against the wall to the left, she also created space to move and sit at the fireside.

On this page, two thoroughly crisp and modern ways of integrating fireplaces into a scheme are shown: below, left and right, very smart bolection moulded fire surrounds contain modern steel grates, while right is a polished Directoire insert, based on a historical design.

Traditional Fireplaces

From the time when fires moved from the centre of a dwelling to an exterior wall with a flue to allow smoke to escape, people began to 'decorate' the surrounding area. From simple painted designs grew some of the most extraordinary architectural masterpieces in marble, stone and elaborately carved wood. Traditional fireplaces can almost be read like a book, identified from country to country by their shape, size and the type of material used.

Original fire surrounds, where they have survived the depredations of fashion, are prized, but such is the choice of reproductions that virtually any style can be found or made. Opposite (top left and bottom right) are two examples of stone and marble architectural fire surrounds, similar in style because both are in old Antwerp houses. Today there is renewed respect for the old styles, even within contemporary interiors.

Large Fireplaces

Fans of French interiors, including – at least in old houses – the French penchant for large fireplaces, will recognize the several examples shown here. Made from cut stone or plastered and painted masonry, they have great appeal – as demonstrated by the fact that reclaimed antique examples appear in houses all over the world. Styles and stone quality vary from region to region, and these fireplaces are often monumental in size, harking back to a time when the fire was the only source of heat for cooking and warmth.

Below, left, the owners of a South African game lodge took a vernacular cue and built massive stone columns in which to site fireplaces. Organic, rough-cut local stone is perfect in a 'bush' setting, even if, as here, the accommodation is otherwise highly sophisticated and luxurious. By boxing out and exaggerating the size of the chimney-breast in a London terraced home (opposite, bottom left), the owner created a much more contemporary shape than would have been possible with any conventional fire surround.

Chairs as a Feature

A single quirky chair, perhaps an utterly modern design placed in a traditional setting or vice versa, creates surprise and sometimes humour (opposite). Chair-makers have always been the superstars of the furniture world, perhaps none more so than Hans J. Wegner, who has been described as the 'chair-maker of chair-makers': his most famous design, the *Y* chair, became known simply as *The Chair*. Berthold Lubetkin's 1930s cowhide-and-timber chair (opposite, right) was an astonishing innovation, with its extremely low level and depth of seat. In the same apartment is a 1958 Norman Cherner moulded-plywood chair, now one of the most iconic of twentieth-century designs.

Pairs of chairs placed together create a sociable feel: below, the two 1920s leather models, with a fringe attached around the seat, are small scale and add a delicate and decidedly beautiful touch to this eighteenth-century panelled room in east London.

Classic Chairs

Classics are usually defined by enduring good design and proportion, affording perennial visual pleasure. Such qualities are exemplified by vintage chairs that remain in production by popular demand – none more so than the external tubular-steel-frame designs, with deep leather cushions, created by Le Corbusier in the 1920s. B&B Italia has produced furniture, chairs and sofas that became classics almost from the moment they were launched: here (below, left) are chairs from its 'Metropolitan' range, in a house in Spain designed by an Italian architect and almost entirely furnished with B&B pieces. A young London-based designer chose a new classic from Poltrona Frau, its *Don' Do Rocker* (2005), made from curved multi-ply beech, with steamed-oak rockers and leather upholstery.

Chaises Longues

A chaise longue is a cross between a narrow bed and a sofa, a place to recline, relax, read and occasionally nod off. Today, rather than being simply a daytime resting-place in the bedroom, it is also an ideal spot from which to hold long telephone conversations. The styling of chaises longues has changed over several centuries, upholstery has been simplified, and new materials are now used, but in essence the chaise longue remains an attractive and useful addition to any room.

The fabulous moody composition below, a living-room in a London designer's home, features a chaise longue of bed-like proportions, plump and inviting. A piece in an altogether different French-inspired style (right), in the same house, was custom-made for the owner, who prefers to collaborate with craftsmen on commissioned pieces to achieve the exact proportions, quality and look that he requires.

Stools

Handy, portable, light and compact, stools have been in use since time immemorial. Rustic, home-made stools were part of country-cottage life for centuries, and in the 1930s the very modern-looking examples found in Egyptian tombs inspired a revival of similar designs. Other parts of Africa, too, have a great tradition of solid-wood, carved stools, varying in design from country to country.

A real curiosity and perhaps not to everyone's taste, the elephant's-foot stool seen here was a colonial fashion, examples of which can still be found at auctions or in country-house storerooms. As furniture design evolved in Europe, the footstool 'proper', as an extension to chairs, became an accessory, its design co-ordinated to fit the specific chair and upholstered in matching fabric. That tradition is maintained today, although contemporary styles are boxier and often set at a distance from the chair to make an alternative 'coffee table' or to display books.

Small Tables

Small tables, ideally about the same height as the arm of a chair or sofa, are valuable pieces of furniture for all manner of practical uses. They can provide handy sites for reading-lights, bowls of flowers, or books. Additionally, as shown on the right, the placing of such tables can create a barely discernible division between a seating area and the main walkway to reach the rest of the room (in this case, in the London home of an interior designer). In this arrangement, the symmetry is impressive, comprising pairs of chairs as well as tables, together with decorative items, all of them unusual and full of character.

Natural wood blocks, cut, coloured or carved, are modern, stool-like interpretations of side tables. The basket-style small table (below, right) works particularly well with the simple dark chair near by. Small tables also break up empty spaces in a subtle, unobtrusive way, and – like modern lightweight chairs – they can be moved about to accommodate changing needs.

Shelving

A great deal of thought usually goes into shelving, not least concerning the question of what will be housed there, and whether to have straight runs of shelves or grid-like boxes of the same size or of differing heights to accommodate taller items, pictures or vases. With careful planning and design, shelving makes all the difference to the management of the objects in the space.

'Books do furnish a room' is a truism. To accommodate them, shelving can be installed either side of a chimney-breast, as free-standing units, cantilevered or custom-designed to fill entire walls. Purist minimalist designers would have none of this multicoloured clutter, but most homes include books of one sort or another – gardening, hobbies, history, travel or novels. Even today, we are not yet exclusively tied to our laptops or electronic books, and rooms without books can appear lifeless, mere showrooms for furniture.

Shelving

The thatched roof and choice of decorative items indicate that this dramatic living-room-cum-library (left) is in Africa – in fact, in a luxury game lodge on the Botswana border. The use of a diamond-shaped shelving unit was a good idea where the ceiling slopes so acutely, as the pattern of the unit breaks up the lines of the structural poles, and effectively frames the large sofa in front. In a very different scheme (opposite, bottom centre), the empty space beneath a modern, narrow staircase leading from the living-area to the mezzanine level of a London apartment has been employed as bookshelves. This is a brilliant use of a small space that is not deep enough for a home office or utility area, such as traditional staircases can provide.

Shelving solutions can be remarkably dynamic and varied, belying the fact that, on the face of it, a shelf might seem an item of limited design potential. Opposite, bottom right, a block of curvy white shelving boxes, called *Boogie Woogie*, is modern and fun, even if in this case the shape is more important than the storage capacity. The oak shelves in the room shown opposite, top, stop short of the left-hand wall, forming a block of colour above the sofa: architects are particularly good at seeing how to make such a simple and practical fitting work in a different and creative way.

Entertainment
Cinema

The demand for home cinemas, or at least for a cinema experience, exploded in the late 1990s, as digital technology progressed, leaving the slide show and home movies flickering on living-room walls far behind. Electronically operated drop-down screens could be easily fitted, and projector equipment mounted on ceilings or recessed into walls. The home cinema thus moved from temporary quarters in whatever room was deemed the most convenient to a full-blown 'movie' experience with special seating, drinks tables, state-of-the-art lighting and surround sound.

Basements and attics are frequently converted into cinemas: since they often lack much natural light, are tucked away in a less obtrusive part of a house, and can perhaps be more easily soundproofed, they are well suited to such transformations. The cinemas shown here have been fitted out and decorated according to their owners' preference, whether that is for a sleek and contemporary look or, opposite, top, a more old-fashioned experience, where the red velvet curtains are of course a nod to the great cinema drapes of the past.

Entertainment
Television

From the time of their invention in the 1940s, television sets sat on tables or sideboards, more often than not making a large, lumpy focal point in the living-room. But as ownership of a television became common to virtually every household, owners and designers began locking them away in cupboards, hidden from view until required. Recently, the development of the flat-screen model, some versions of which are huge, has had a new impact on the way some living-rooms are designed. The most noticeable difference is the placing of the screen – rather than a mirror or painting – above a fireplace, but, as seen here, it can be positioned anywhere that suits the grouping of furniture provided for the viewers' comfort and sociability. For those people who prefer the screen to disappear when not in use, it is best to mount it on a dark background.

Entertainment
Television

Two of the designs shown here allow for a modern television to be free-standing on top of a piece of furniture, rather than wall mounted. Both form an elegant composition, and the very long unit with a tall lamp placed at each end seems to diminish the impact of the television considerably. Opposite, top, this small living-room-cum-library in a London apartment has the benefit of a dual aspect, but the room is quite narrow, so the designer created a platform extension to the bookshelves.

Below, this rooftop apartment has more glass than wall, but by fitting the television into a corner section of wall, and choosing an L-shaped sofa, the owner has not allowed the set to dominate the space. The centrally placed screen, opposite, bottom, is treated more like a work of art, since the furniture is not grouped around it as the focal point of the space.

Vases

Vases, pots and jugs are highly collectable, functional and fascinating. Made from clay, pots and jugs used for wine, oil and water are some of our oldest domestic goods. As long as it is capable of holding water, any object can be used as a vase. For example, part of a collection of First World War shell cases found on the battlefields of the Somme in France, and curiously similar in colour to a Munyaradzi stone bust from Zimbabwe

(opposite, bottom right), makes unusual flower containers in a London apartment.

In a magnificent *salon marocain* (above), part of a modern house outside Marrakesh, the owner collects old pots and vases that were made locally or near by. The walls of the room are earth-coloured, as is the pottery, which is made in Marrakesh. On a low stone-topped table in Provence (opposite, bottom left), a celadon-green container is just the right choice for displaying scented dried lavender once the fresh variety has

finished. The pair of tall vases atop an antique cupboard (opposite, top left) creates a pleasing vertical line in the living-room of a French country house, the owners of which also spend time in Asia, collecting all manner of interesting decorative objects and textiles to integrate into their home.

Busts and Statues

Busts and statues have adorned our lives for thousands of years. Think of the great stone statues of ancient Egypt, Greece and Rome, and the political and military heroes of more recent centuries who gaze upon us from plinths high above our pavements. People collect every sort of human and religious form there has ever been, from tiny fertility symbols to over-life-size, often headless, torsos. Asian carvings and sculpture, whether wood, bronze, brass or silver, have always held great appeal in the West, an attraction that frequently goes far beyond the simply spiritual. Enigmatic and inscrutable, such statues can be very beautiful and calming.

Antiquity has also given us a wealth of fine sculpture made from marble, bone, ivory, gilded and painted wood, and clay. Today, glass, resin, paper and plaster are likewise used in highly creative ways to produce a modern version of a most ancient art form.

Halls and Stairways

The provision of adequate, even generous transitional spaces in homes is of some importance regarding how well and how comfortably we live. Entrance halls, large or small, give a promise of what is to come, and provide a brief moment to settle as the door closes behind us. Not all halls contain stairs, but where they do, the design and construction of a staircase can be a major architectural feature and a thing of great beauty. Broad, well-lit, shallow treads leading gently upwards; sinuous, curving and shell-like structures; or a linear series of blocks devoid of rails and decoration, staircases can create grandeur or utilitarian simplicity. Landings at each level are important in the separation of spaces; stairs that lead directly into rooms can be intrusive, requiring the movement of people through the room to reach another level, and this may cause problems with furniture placement where such a 'corridor' for access is required.

The amount of space allocated for transition is a much-debated subject among architects, designers and their clients. Fear that all that 'wasted' space could be better employed for living is a common misconception, although as urban apartments, in particular, become smaller, designers are responding to the challenge by devising some very clever solutions, especially where lack of natural light is concerned, often involving a canny choice of materials. Where no entrance hall or lobby exists, a simple panel, perhaps on a pivot, can provide an all-important screen and momentary transition from the entrance into the rest of the home.

Curving Staircases

The best way to appreciate the design and beauty of a staircase is by looking down from the top level in order to understand the shape and how the return at each change of level works. One of the most dramatic staircase designs includes double landings, lit by tall windows and perhaps a roof lantern, and giving access to rooms on both sides.

Banisters of every conceivable shape and size were used to support handrails until about the 1640s, when panels of cut-out decoration became fashionable, but the cycle of prevailing fashions is ever-changing. Rigorous attention to detail was undertaken by the designer of this new house in central London (opposite, top right), where the banisters are not fussy but have gentle curves that create fluidity of line. The balustrade is made of hand-forged iron, bronzed and finished in gold leaf; the handrail is of honey-stained maple, and the stairs themselves are made of French limestone.

The Georgian staircase (opposite, bottom left and right) is a much more oval shape, splaying at hall level but without newel posts, which creates a very lightweight appearance. The Modernist concrete design in a Provençal warehouse conversion (right) takes up the minimum amount of space, the circular form appearing sculptural.

Curving Staircases

If a broad spiral or semi-spiral staircase is the most sinuous and exciting architectural form, there are others of equal, more discreet beauty, with gentler curves. On these pages, it is interesting to note that all but the staircase shown opposite, bottom right, are French. The odd one out is a survivor of a typical London terraced-house style; the banisters may be plainer than usual, but the mahogany handrail shows a touch of refinement.

In France, glorious ironwork was favoured, and in new houses there, designers still go to great lengths to reinterpret old designs, inspired by the numerous patterns and fine craftsmanship for which France is famous. There is a great variety in stair-tread design, depending on tradition and local materials. Among the many possibilities are stone topped with tile and timber nosing; solid stone or oak; patterned tiles; steel; or glass, as we shall see later (pages 80–81).

Straight Staircases

The architect–owner of this house in southern Spain (above) built his house to reflect the local vernacular and to provide enough wall space to display an important collection of modern art. The entrance is at first-floor level, with bridges to the left and to the right, off which run two straight stone staircases to the ground floor.

In a Marrakesh riad, where the living-space occupies the central courtyard, a narrow concrete staircase leads up to mezzanine landings on two sides of the house and thence up to the roof terrace. Finished in charcoal polished plaster, the steps are particularly sculptural when seen against a creamy, mellow brick wall. The limed-oak staircase (opposite) is generous in size, yet does not dominate the wide but low-ceilinged entrance hall. The floors, walls and timber are all of a similar light and neutral colour, helping to reduce the impact of the staircase.

Staircase Materials

A staircase can be made of anything that will carry weight and is properly structurally supported. The sheer simplicity of these glass treads (below, left), set in polished-plaster walls and appearing to float in mid-air, is spectacular, although not for the faint-hearted or those prone to vertigo. Tight spiral staircases can be placed anywhere in a room, and were traditionally made of painted iron. In a German house (right), the steel spiral has been placed in a half-column of curved steel panelling. It is a modern design with factory or industrial roots.

Opposite, right, instead of banisters and obvious handrails, flat sheets of metal bolted on to unseen newel posts form a solid protection for the wooden stairs; the design echoes the bolted-timber construction of the house. Formed of brick or concrete and plastered and painted, these white staircases (far right and opposite, left) possess a pristine, uncomplicated beauty. Both are in houses near the sea, the first on the east coast of Spain, and the second on the southern French coast. The supremely elegant curving steps (below, right), leading from the house through a tunnel to a pool hall, take their form from the circular roof-light above the lobby area.

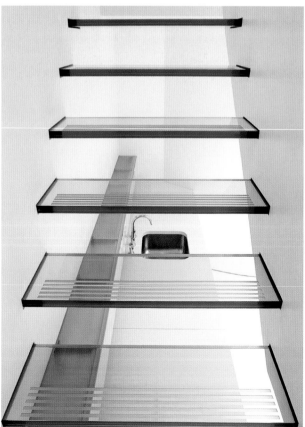

Tiled Floors

Entrance-hall floors need to be tough. Whether ceramic or stone, marble or concrete, tiles are chosen because they are the most hard-wearing surface, impervious to wet feet, umbrellas or damp dogs. In an early house by Edwin Lutyens (opposite, left), the designer who undertook the three-year refurbishment looked to Lutyens's original use of materials when choosing a mix of polished and honed Purbeck marble flooring in the library hall and for the replacement fireplaces.

Old French country houses traditionally had stone-flagged halls (as did English ones), although ceramic tiles later became popular. Below, right, this 1930s Lubetkin-designed apartment in north London looks so contemporary. The square brown floor tiles used both for the entry steps and in the small lobby area seen here are crisp and modern, as are the wide timber wall cladding and pivoting shutters.

Wooden Floors

In apartments it makes sense to use the same flooring throughout, especially where the accommodation is largely open plan and on one level, or where there is no definite entrance hall. In a house, where there is more space, stone or tile can be chosen for the entrance-hall floor, but throughout the rest of the house, including corridors, landings and halls, timber is a fine material. Ranging from almost white to black, reclaimed, fired, new or specially coloured, it is superbly versatile. Laid as parquet blocks, seen here with a colourful oriental rug in Morocco (far right), or with the marked grain used to create a pattern in a Spanish apartment (right), it affords many possibilities.

Below, right, the German firm of Schotten and Hansen supplied this richly coloured oak flooring for a modern house in southern Spain. Opposite, an eighteenth-century house in Spitalfields, east London, retains its old floorboards, regardless of the fact that they no longer lie flush to one another. The precious patina of such boards is almost impossible to replicate.

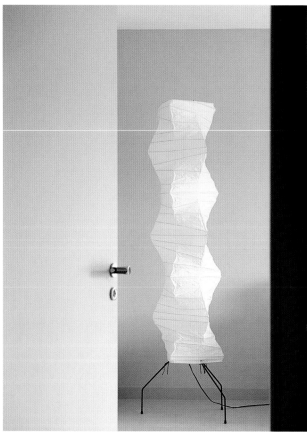

Lights

Lighting a stairwell is quite different from lighting other parts of the house. Traditionally, carriage lanterns hung from chains were popular, dropping through the void from floor to floor. Halls may feature a combination of ceiling pendants and wall lights, multiples of a single style, or, in the case of the low ceiling shown opposite, top right, a broad but shallow, circular glass fitting designed by Mark Brazier Jones for a client who is also an interior designer. It is an exciting choice in an extremely glamorous entrance hall.

Opposite, top left, the owner–designer of a modern house in Marrakesh found an original Verner Panton chandelier, a 1960s design from the 'Fun Shell' range, semi-translucent and lustrous, created from layers of sliced shells. High ceilings allow for such elongated designs as this. A line of similar but not identical pendant lights with French-inspired metal shades has been hung along an open corridor in a South African game lodge. The look is artisan and handmade, well suited to the mix of rustic and highly sophisticated interior finishes in this suite of rooms.

Wall Mirrors

Mirror glass, framed or not, or cut and applied as mosaic or strips, creates fabulous results – expanding any space, reflecting light, adding glamour and frequently producing interesting vistas. A warehouse-conversion entrance hall, right, was transformed by a London designer for his client by applying 12,000 pieces of mosaic mirror glass to the wall in a slightly uneven fashion. The reflection possesses something of the look of an Impressionist painting.

Opposite, right, at basement level, the designer–owner used mirror panels not only to enhance the space leading to the bedrooms, but also effectively to increase the sense of natural light. In an entirely contemporary rooftop apartment in London (below, right), a gigantic antique-framed mirror is propped against the hall wall, creating a perfect contrast between the poured-cement floors and the ornate gilt frame. Opposite, left, during the complete refurbishment of a Huf house in Germany, the designer improved a small entrance lobby by virtually filling one wall with a backlit mirror.

Dark Colours

On the basis that it is difficult to create additional natural light where there is already only little, halls and windowless entrance spaces can be decorated in the deepest tones without fear of looking inappropriately gloomy. On the other hand, a well-lit entrance, such as the one featured opposite, right, can nonetheless be given a shady, cool atmosphere, created here by the choice of polished black floors and a dark palm-trunk ceiling.

A light-coloured, fabric-tented ceiling and contrasting collection of folk-costume illustrations, mounted and framed in off-white, transform a very dark-grey entrance into a lively space, heightening the expectation of what is to follow. Again, in the scheme above, the success lies in the contrast: deep Prussian-blue walls combine well with a corn-coloured carpet, a white bust and a gilt picture-frame. Opposite, left, a monumental polished-plaster tunnel heralds the entrance to a modern house in

Marrakesh, designed by Jean-François Zevaco. Dark and moody, providing ideal shelter in such a hot climate, it propels the visitor through the dimly lit space and forward into the welcoming light of the interior.

Various Colours

An entrance hall or lobby may be a contained space that does not visually link to the rest of the house, and in such cases the hall can be treated to an individual colour scheme. Opposite, the owner–designer of a classic English country house has used yellow and white for the entrance, inner lobby and staircase; it would have been confusing to change wall colour in such an open, flowing space.

The vivid palette of pink and orange chosen by the owners for their Legorreta-designed house in Spain reflects both local tradition and the owners' interest in and work with colour. It is usual to continue a single colour from the bottom to the top of a staircase, but a subtle change of tone from dark to light is effective in creating a feeling of upward progression.

Floor and Wall Patterns

None of these images shows conventional wall or floor treatments. A London gardener has lined the walls and ceilings of his small hallway with modern maps, a sort of contemporary take, with a difference, on the 'print room'. The over-scaled tulips, opposite, top right, were painted by the owner directly on to the staircase walls of a house in Antwerp; he is a garden designer with a passion for old tulip varieties, and has become something of an expert. The exquisite geometric floor pattern in Purbeck marble, with a mirrored centre reflecting a domed ceiling and oculus (opposite, bottom right), was created by a leading London designer for an English country house.

The setting of river pebbles into concrete floors in a South African game lodge (opposite, bottom left) created a simple, rustic floor pattern, one based on very old traditions. Right, in a Spanish villa, both the architecture and all the interior finishes were inspired by Tuscan design; this floor, made of Spanish marble, was laid by Italian craftsmen from drawings made by the Marbella-based interior designer.

Monochrome Wall Patterns

Three very different effects have been created in these halls, although each one is treated to a calm, pale colour scheme into which very dark contrasting elements have been added. The arabesque shapes used in a London warehouse apartment (opposite, left) could have been flamboyant or busy, but by keeping to an off-white colour scheme given a tougher look by the inclusion of a patinated steel-clad door, the designer reflected the apartment's former origins most effectively. The architect–owner of a north London cottage dating from the early twentieth century (opposite, right) used a subtle gold-and-cream paper on one wall. Barely visible during daytime, the pattern comes alive at night. By painting the staircase black, the owner avoided any blandness and lifted the space into contemporary mode very easily.

It is a tenet in decorating that the use of horizontal stripes – left, in a short entrance hall in Marrakesh – gives a sense of elongation in a small space. The polished-plaster stripes – simply a change of texture – seen here on a flat painted wall of the same colour are a low-key but chic decorating detail.

Patterned Runners, Rugs and Cushions

Small grey linen cushions printed with the hand of Fatima (to avert the evil eye) have been placed on the staircase of a Marrakesh riad (opposite, left) – a pleasing and stylish detail that is appropriate to the location. This symbol can be seen on walls and tiles throughout Morocco.

Carpet runners bring colour, pattern and warmth to hall floors. Grand old houses seem to suit faded and worn rugs, looking as if they have been in place for hundreds of years. In this exceptional Irish castle entrance hall (right), the young owners inherited some of the contents, including the large oriental rug. The stairs, too, feature a narrow floral carpet, useful for softening the sound of footsteps on the wooden treads.

While owners of modern apartments do not eschew antique carpets entirely, the long striped rug seen here in Brussels (below, right) perfectly anchors the disparate mix of art and furniture in the hall of the bedroom wing.

Chairs

The wider the landing, hall or corridor, the easier it is to furnish as a living-space rather than as just a transitional, walk-through access-way. The contemporary mezzanine (above), using glass and metal, perfectly illustrates the consideration given to how furniture might be placed; the Le Corbusier chair teamed with a Cattelani & Smith floor lamp, and room for books and pictures, eliminates any feeling of wasted space.

Chairs in halls can be low and comfortable, upright and practical, or simply a favourite singleton, such as the demi-lune Swedish painted chair (opposite, bottom left) on which to leave a coat or scarf. The Anglo-German owners of a French country house with two halls (opposite, top left and right) have mixed Victorian needlepoint with Chinese elm chairs and French ironwork. In another house, opposite, bottom right, the small cane-backed chair does not project beyond the hall console table, leaving a clear passage through from the entrance.

Chairs

In the eighteenth and nineteenth centuries, 'hall' chairs were of solid mahogany construction, often with carved shield backs – in grander houses, the owner's coat of arms might be included – and were placed in a line along the hall wall to seat waiting visitors. This arrangement had nothing to do with comfort; those who used such chairs were perfectly well aware of the hierarchical social system that was in play. Manners and etiquette have

changed, but some fine examples of these chairs survive (above, left), and work as well in halls today as they ever did.

A chair upholstered in bright or unusual fabric brings colour and form into an otherwise unfurnished corridor or hall (opposite, bottom centre); the beech-framed red and orange chairs (above, right) liven up a modern concrete staircase in a very old house in Germany. Bedroom landings and halls suit larger, softer models, such as the white upholstered chair (opposite, top).

Sofas and Settees

Chosen for its looks, form or scale rather than purely for comfort, a sofa or bench is a lovely addition to a spacious hall or landing. Modern or antique, sculptural or plump, it provides colour and shape in what may otherwise be an empty walkway. A narrow seat is the main consideration, but the placing of the small-scale, upright green sofa precisely in the centre of the landing (opposite, bottom) adds drama and focus to a quite austere symmetrical space; the curves of the arms and legs of the sofa also cleverly echo the wavy banisters of the staircase. The sofa, which dates from about 1715, has its original gilt finish and is upholstered in shimmering green silk velvet.

Slim modern benches with cushioned seats subtly break up the lines of the very tall windows and doorcase in a spacious London house (opposite, top right); elsewhere, the use of a smart blue-and-white-striped fabric gives a contemporary feel to a painted Regency cane sofa in London.

Tables

Tables can serve many practical and aesthetic functions when placed in a hall. Entrance halls, in particular, should ideally include a surface on which keys or the daily newspaper can be put. In large halls, a centrally placed table also breaks up what may be an awkward space, and provides the ideal setting for a welcoming display of flowers.

Pretty, wall-mounted iron consoles were chosen both for a London family home (opposite, top left) and by a designer who wished to add interest to the lobby area giving access to his bedrooms. Placing a table against a wall also provides a framework for display. Pictures, books, sculpture or a hunting trophy – that most traditional of country-house objects – can form an interesting or amusing tableau in what may otherwise be a little-noticed space. Above, right, a massive jar, made into a table by placing a glass disc on its top, is

a neat and inventive way to soften the strict symmetry of this hall in Surrey without appearing to take up much space.

Tables

In a very tight space, such as this old staircase in northern France (opposite, right), the perfect solution to creating a small display area was a corner table, in this case a wonderfully worn little piece that works very well with the distressed-blue walls.

In the London home of an interior designer and antiques dealer, a pair of old chimney pots topped with a rugged piece of stone forms a charming and original hall table. Such a piece can take the knocks of daily comings and goings far better than a precious antique specimen. Hall tables are seldom square; the size and shape of the space usually dictate that a round or rectangular table is more suitable. A table with a mirror or favourite picture placed above it works particularly well; likewise, the size and faded colouring of the painted cloth (probably from a theatre set) that fills the wall behind the chimney-pot table make it a highly effective choice.

Art Objects

Art objects cover a vast range of styles, materials, sizes and subjects, but in the home, pieces are generally chosen because of an association or the desire to create a certain 'look'. Plaster or marble busts of Greek or Roman worthies or beauties immediately lend a Classical feel to any room, and this works particularly well where a single piece stands alone in a hall (opposite, bottom right). In a Spanish apartment, the bronze Pierrot (opposite, left) looks stunning as a result of being lit by a window behind, framed by glossy silk curtains.

Opposite, top right, an interior designer has a wonderful mix of art and objects in his London riverside apartment. The crackle-glaze vase from Paris, placed below a wall-mounted mask, creates an interesting mix of cultures, shapes and colours. Neptune, standing proud in a Brussels staircase (below, left), was left in the house by the former owner, while (right) one might presume a cat-lover chose the exquisite life-like stainless-steel leaping feline placed on a hall table. The sculpture's impact is dramatically doubled by being reflected in the large mirror behind it.

Miscellaneous Objects

It might seem odd to place an old-fashioned stove in a small hall between two much larger rooms, but this ancient house in Burgundy (opposite, left) is full of such quirky puzzles. The main rooms are blessed with enormous fireplaces, and, as the house is now used only in the summer, no modern heating has been installed. It is rare to find such an untouched beauty.

Many of us find that books are taking over our lives, so this English cottage staircase is a sensible place to stack them up, giving easy access to the titles as well as visual pleasure every day.

Like books, collections seem to grow and fill every possible space. A set of shallow, Directoire-style shelving tucked beside the staircase, above, left, stores a great variety of old books, boots, seals, busts, pots and boxes. Opposite, right, a London tailor has placed an old shop unit on a landing in his Georgian house to display a range of shirts; the house effectively doubles as his home and atelier.

Miscellaneous Objects

A hall can be the ideal place to display less conventional, striking objects. The double-volume space created in a Provençal warehouse conversion (opposite, right) allowed the owner–designer to display a cherished model of an American P51 Mustang (his passions are vintage cars, motorbikes and aircraft). A child-size racing car is displayed on the ground floor (opposite, left).

Country houses often have several entrance halls, one of which, probably close to the kitchen, is used on a daily basis for storing boots, wet-weather gear, baskets and dog-leads. Hampers of firewood and fir cones, perhaps too rustic for the living-room, are attractive additions to a stone-floored hall. Right, hunting trophies mounted above doors and along hall walls are frequently seen in German, French and English houses, even where the current owners are not hunters themselves. Many fine specimens, marked with the name of a previous generation and the date of the shoot, are inherited.

Kitchens

Kitchens have come full circle. Through many generations, the kitchen evolved from a single living-space with a fire to a purpose-built room set away from the heart of the house, or a utilitarian space added to the back. Today, however, the kitchen is once more a living-room, and indeed the focal point or hub of most homes. No matter the size of a house or apartment, architects, designers and owners know that a good deal of daily life will be spent in the kitchen. As a result, the design and manufacture of modern kitchens have become increasingly complex, not because we cook more, but because we instinctively gravitate to where food and drink are served. And, as we now demand numerous aids beyond the simple supply of heat and water, the machinery of the kitchen – whether hidden away (urban style) or more unfitted with open shelving (country style) – has become highly sophisticated. Even the most inexperienced cook will often acquire a formidable *batterie de cuisine*, along with a collection of recipe books, a large fridge, coffee machine, microwave oven, dishwasher and an all-important, state-of-the-art extraction system. A smart or designer kitchen has become a key selling-point in any property, although, paradoxically, kitchens are now subject to such rapidly changing fashions that they are ripped out and replaced at an extraordinary – some might say, profligate – rate. Most kitchens are, by necessity, 'modern': the principal differences thus lie largely in the prevailing decorative style, the choice of materials and, to a lesser degree, colour and display. There is a huge variety, but the kitchens chosen for this book demonstrate both current trends and the great individuality that can be applied to the hardest-working room in the house.

Urban

Characterized by smooth, often seamless surfaces, and more drawers than cupboards, the urban kitchen – of any size – appears to be both more customized and minimal in terms of style, and usually contains the most up-to-date equipment. Increasingly, where space allows, wall-mounted cupboards are excluded, and gas or electric hobs are set directly into the work surface. Ovens and microwaves are built into

walls of storage that may extend from floor to ceiling, appearing more architectural than traditional standard designs. Curtains or blinds, if used at all, are kept extremely simple, and for work areas such materials as Corian, stainless steel and glass are preferred to wood. In the quest for simplicity of line, taps are pared down to a single column, while knobs and handles have all but disappeared.

Urban

White kitchen units and walls could be described as 'classic' urban style. Whether hand-painted or applied in a sprayed gloss finish, white is a fashionable but enduring scheme, and the easiest 'colour' to live with. Teamed with stainless-steel detailing in everything from the slimmest of drawer handles to each kitchen appliance, white gives the impression not only of greater hygiene but also of a particular purity – as evinced in innumerable bathrooms, where gleaming white porcelain baths and basins are deployed to pristine effect. Reflective surfaces are more popular in genuinely urban kitchens than in the country, probably because town and city kitchens often enjoy less natural light. White also contrasts well with a multitude of other materials, such as black granite work surfaces, or can be used to complement others, such as limed-oak floorboards. For a truly urban look, white resin floors – although high maintenance – are the ultimate in clean living.

Urban

An urban-style kitchen does not have to be in a city-centre house, and does not rely on modern architecture for its context. Some of the most impressive contemporary kitchens are to be found in old houses with high ceilings, panelled doors and sash windows.

The kitchens shown here are set in homes that include a 'new-build' Victorian home (opposite, top), a Hampstead cottage (below, left) and a grand Georgian house (below, right). All are distinctly urban, the common factor being that each uses an island unit either to divide the working and cooking areas in an open-plan kitchen, or to create additional work surfaces. In the Georgian house, there is more than a nod to the unfitted kitchens of the past, but the materials – steel and stone – are uncompromisingly modern.

Country

Just as urban style can work in a country house, country style may be applied in city homes, but not in the same way that the country look flourished during the 1980s. Then, every surface was crowded with jugs and dried flowers, while walls were filled with garlands, pictures and plate racks. Now, however, the style has been simplified. Wooden work surfaces, belfast sinks, open shelving and range cookers create a country look, but excessive clutter has largely disappeared.

Contrary to appearances, two of these three kitchens are in cities. Below, the painted beamed ceiling instantly provides a country feel, but in fact this kitchen is in London; opposite, an Antwerp town house features a country-style kitchen. The warm colours, tiled floor and antique furniture in the charming painted kitchen (right) are reliable indicators that this house is in Provence. For the country style, scrubbed-pine or old-stone floors are much more convincing than concrete, resin or modern tiles. The look is casual and lived-in – and, essentially, the cook's tools are on display.

Country

In three of these kitchens, the cooker is housed, as the very early models were, within what was or might have been a chimney-breast. Simple, glass-shaded pendant lamps hark back to the first electric lights, and the framed cupboards are made in a traditional way. In the country style, oiled-hardwood work surfaces remain popular, and slate or zinc are more likely to be used than in the urban look. The country-house-style kitchen continues to be updated, but the magnificent 1950s Aga seen here (opposite, bottom right) was not replaced by a modern steel range cooker; an Aga is the most 'country' sort of cooker and has maintained its status as a firm favourite. It is more difficult to define the look precisely as urban and country merge, but other typical characteristics of this style are mismatched furniture and – thanks to the prominence of the oven and the open display of utensils, bowls of fruit and herbs – a strong sense that the room is a working kitchen, a place where real cooking occurs.

Country

Modern country-style kitchens often borrow simple features from the past, such as wall-mounted shelves to house ingredients and utensils that are regularly used, but the difference is that the containers on display are not haphazard. For example, the pots and pans may vary in size, but not in design or quality, and the kitchen is likely to have about it an air of professional orderliness. Similarly, there will often be a mix of modern and antique furniture and lighting, but the whole set-up will have been planned in much greater detail, not allowing for the random acquisition of ornaments, vases, knick-knacks or much in the way of decorative items. Today's country kitchens, whether located in a farmhouse or city-centre home, are likely to be just as well – and as consciously – designed as their urban counterparts.

Display

Even in contemporary kitchens, there are those who prefer to see their utensils, cookery books, favourite china and travel mementoes on show. Items put on display in kitchens often vary greatly from those in the rest of the house, and may range from the purely decorative and pleasing to the eye to the entirely practical, but in each case there is a story behind or resonance in the choice. Pictures, artefacts and lamps all indicate that the kitchen is treated as much as a living-space as as a cooking arena – a place that is an expression of its owner's interests. For those who like empty work surfaces, bare walls and a planned storage space for absolutely everything, 'display' is often synonymous with 'clutter', but the busier look is often undeniably interesting, definitely extremely personal and, as we shall see overleaf, capable of greatly enhancing the beauty and appeal of the room.

Display

The French country kitchen (above)
is a classic example of everyday
kitchenware displayed with an eye
to the beauty of the objects. In each
kitchen shown here, open shelving,
rather than cupboards, has been chosen
not only to provide storage but also to
create, in different ways, an attractive
'soft-edged' approach to kitchen style.
Die-hard minimalists would argue that
the effect is messy or difficult to keep
clean, but for the owners, the fact that
plates, cookery books and utensils
can all be appreciated and are
within easy reach is well worth any
maintenance involved.

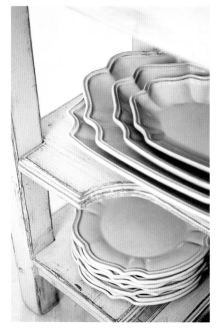

Display

By design, the most contemporary kitchens may limit any display to a few purely practical items, such as kettles and toasters, but many people enjoy seeing such decorative and useful objects as plates, bowls, decanters, glasses and teapots. There are simply no rules about what to show off in a kitchen, and some people treat theirs as another living-room or a picture gallery. Above, the array of individually painted figurative tiles

behind the taps is unusual, but since there is little risk of them being damaged by water, they make a very striking display.

Opposite, bottom, this kitchen belonging to a top British chef and cookery writer includes a display of white bowls, jugs, a bread bin and simple glassware that is pleasing to the eye. The owner has an adjacent walk-in pantry and storage room, so the kitchen is not too crammed with the tools of his trade. Opposite, top right, the old dresser in a

very large country kitchen is the most classic and traditional of all pieces of kitchen furniture. Packed with old-fashioned china and other collectables, it creates an undeniably charming look. It may not prove practical to display so many things, however, and the decision will depend on the amount and type of cooking that take place in the space.

Storage

A key component in any kitchen design is storage: the need to house a multitude of items that vary greatly in size, shape and use. Over the centuries, many options have been devised, but the choice largely depends on the space available. An entire other room – the pantry – was the perfect solution when kitchens were 'unfitted' and equipment limited. Now that we have so many appliances, modern kitchens are planned so that maximum storage is created, with the fridge replacing cool marble shelves; unit drawers designed to carry the weight of stacked china or heavy pans; and the slimmest of wall-mounted cupboards made in such a way as to contain effectively all the 'store-cupboard' essentials.

The way in which storage solutions work best is highly individual. In a new twist, two very different pieces of furniture – an antique writing-desk and a glossy black cabinet – have been used to store glass and china; both pieces are slightly removed from the working part of the kitchen. Whether open or closed storage, displayed or hidden containers, solid cupboard doors or – as seen here in a house in Marrakesh – traditional moucharaby openwork panels (right), the choice is apparently limitless.

Storage

Shallow glazed cupboards, their shelves just wide enough to store a single stack of plates, bowls or jugs, create a practical country look. Practical, because the contents can be seen easily, and there is no need to search the backs of deep cupboards for infrequently used kitchen ingredients or china. The style of the cupboard doors, whether part panelled or fully glazed, can be made to match existing windows or any other architectural details in the house. Instead of clear glass, mirror panels are sometimes used, thereby apparently expanding the space, and reflecting light.

By contrast, where symmetry is not important, solid wooden cupboards filling an entire wall (opposite, bottom) work well; being narrow, this style of storage has a more discreet effect in the room, especially when painted the same colour as the walls. If the tops of the cupboards finish below ceiling height, there is plenty of space to display decorative pieces, vases and candlesticks – things that are not in daily use, but are good to look at.

Storage

As we have already seen (pages 118–119), urban kitchen storage tends to be fully fitted, filling every inch of space from floor to ceiling, and using a single finish or mixing lacquer with wood, or glass with steel. For the purist, there can be not a single item on display (below, left); specially designed drawers contain compartments for everything from individual carving knives to the lemon squeezer.

Purpose-built wine cellars – temperature-controlled, humid and well lit – have become very popular, and can be created in odd spaces other than the traditional, cool, underground cellar (opposite). For serious wine-lovers with plenty of space, designers and specialist joiners can build not only bottle storage but also seating, tasting-tables, and drawers and shelves to hold all the accoutrements a wine buff is bound to collect.

Materials
Stone and Marble

Stone, marble, granite and concrete – so numerous are the colours, patterns and finishes available that kitchens, and indeed bathrooms, are often designed around the choice of material, setting the scene for the rest of the space. Neutral, cream-coloured stone, sometimes used for flooring as well as work surfaces, creates a calm, light backdrop to timber or stainless-steel kitchen furniture. Where very large, seamless surfaces are required, concrete can be tinted to resemble stone (opposite, top left). Honed, hammered or highly polished, figured or not, stone is tough, durable and beautiful; when quarried locally, it makes the perfect choice for both modern and traditional kitchens.

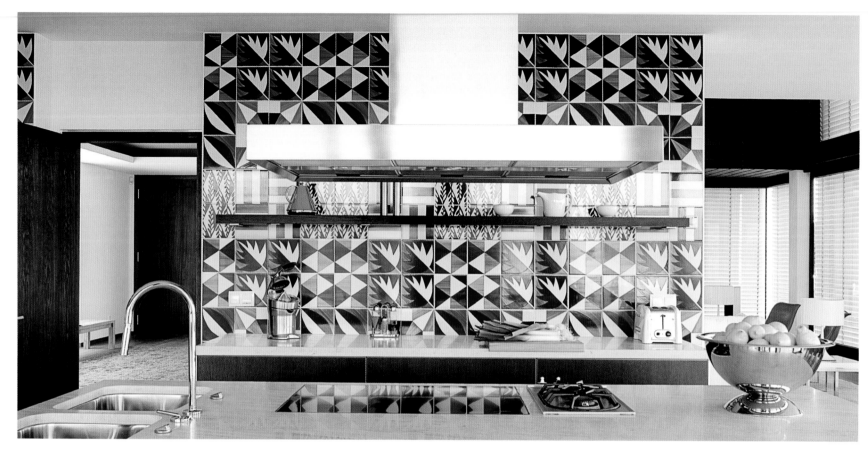

Materials
Tiles

One can journey through history by studying tiles, and virtually every country has a tradition of tile-making. Usually made in small-scale, craft industries, tiles have existed for millennia, their decoration a matter of cultural influences, artistic fervour or simply the pigments that were available with which to create glazes. The nationality of a kitchen can often be recognized instantly from the choice of wall or countertop tiles. The wall of blue-and-white tiles above was specially designed for a house in Spain, while, right, a Provençal kitchen has tiles from the famous tile-producing town of Apt.

As these four examples show, tiles come in all shapes and sizes. Some are rustic, others glossy and white, pearlized. Whatever their style or colour, and whether they are hand-painted or incised, they can be used on the diagonal, in straight lines or to create stripes, as well as a myriad of other geometric or patterning effects.

Materials
Wood

Painted or unpainted wood is versatile, renewable and durable. The millions of pine kitchens fitted in recent decades have survived because, as fashion moved on – and, with it, the rustic wood kitchen – the fittings could easily be repainted, bleached, sand-blasted, polished, lacquered or clad with other material. Similarly, hardwood kitchen worktops can take a beating, and burn marks may be sanded away. Exotic wood veneers are available (above, right) in a wide variety of patterns and grains, and in colours ranging through many shades, from almost black to white. One of the most enduring styles for wooden fittings is painted tongue-and-groove panels. These may be equally effective in creating a country style, when painted in a distressed finish (opposite, bottom left), or – when treated to a high-gloss paint and chrome handles – an entirely urban one.

Multiple Lighting

Lighting, particularly in kitchens, has become a great deal more studied. As a result, it is now not only more stylish, but also entirely specific to the tasks and way of life associated with the room. The use of multiple light fittings – in pairs, in lines or angled over a specific surface – creates a cohesive look, especially where cooking and dining take place in the same room. Very large chrome-and-glass fittings (opposite, left) appear semi-industrial and modern, while spotlights, placed at the correct distance apart, wash walls and work surfaces effectively (above), particularly where only one area requires light, rather than the entire space being lit up by single switching.

Statement Lighting

Pendant lighting and table lamps were banished from kitchens for many years, but both have made a comeback. Strip lights mounted beneath wall cupboards were practical, if a little dull, but the creative process has moved on, especially where lighting a free-standing work surface or dining-table is concerned.

Ceiling downlighters, even dimmable fittings, were usually fixed too high. Recent trends have emerged in which lowered lighting, echoing the shape of the work area or table (right), is popular. Ranging from custom-made (and often designed around an extractor) to an antique chandelier, and from contemporary porcelain to retro Scandinavian fittings, lowered lighting breaks up the monotony of ceilings and focuses light on to specific areas. A table lamp placed on a kitchen counter (opposite, bottom left) adds a softer touch to an otherwise hard-working, granite-topped surface.

Dining

Rooms dedicated solely to dining are a fairly recent development, one that peaked in the nineteenth century and began declining in the late twentieth. Without staff, many dining-rooms became impractical, being too far from the kitchen, too formal, and ending up as simply wasted space, used perhaps only at Christmas or for other important family occasions. As greater space was given to kitchens, often by removing a wall between the two rooms, open-plan kitchen-dining and living-dining became popular, if not essential, especially in smaller homes. The task of cooking and serving food is now generally no longer a solitary business, even when guests are invited. On the following pages we have included kitchen-dining and living-dining rooms, furnished and decorated in both traditional and modern styles, as well as rooms dedicated only to dining – but the trend is definitely for more sociable, connected spaces.

In a room reserved exclusively for dining, the decoration and colour scheme need not link in any way to the rest of the house. Deep-red or deep-green walls, damask and wallpaper, panelling and portraits were once the hallmarks of a formal dining-space. Now, where cooking, eating and living take place in a fully or partially open-plan area, much greater consideration is given to informality and continuity of design. Whether the style is urbane or traditional, there is less division of space by colour, finish, flooring or style of furniture and choice of fabric. While strong colour has not disappeared completely, it is clear that the favoured choice of the new century continues to be pale and interesting. Meanwhile, the dining-table is likely to be the most flexible item of furniture one owns, doing duty by turns as a desk, a food-preparation or play surface, and, best of all, a venue for good conversation.

Kitchen-Dining
Contemporary

Contemporary dining, even though it might include antiques or a free-standing storage unit (below), is a different sort of experience from the traditional, softer-edged approach. Typically, contemporary tables will be made of colder surfaces, such as glass, stainless steel, marble or stone, rather than mahogany or pine. Contemporary designs, in which tables have been reduced in construction to the extent that they appear to have little support, married with vintage pieces by such famous names as Saarinen or Eames, conjure up a powerful sense of modernity. Other details seen on these pages, such as the two fireplaces, each stripped to an undecorated 'fire-box' in the wall; the lack of carpets or rugs; the choice of lighting; and the overall emphasis on spareness and functionality, all indicate a contemporary dining look, chosen to harmonize with the latest in kitchen design and style.

Kitchen-Dining
Contemporary

These two kitchen-dining rooms have much in common, although the first (right) is in London and the second (opposite) near St-Rémy-de-Provence in France. Both are in small warehouse conversions, the first of which, with the added advantage of its dual-aspect situation, was made into a number of apartments, while the other is a single house with a courtyard garden. Dark, metal-framed windows are a shared feature, as is the neutral, almost entirely black-and-white colour scheme. Both properties are owned and were designed by men who are designers themselves, one a craftsman who designs and makes beautiful lighting, the other an architectural and restoration specialist with a penchant for Modernism with a soft edge. As one might expect, both schemes are confident, comfortable and practical.

Kitchen-Dining
Traditional

In relation to these images, the term 'traditional' is used to denote a look: each room is furnished with old tables and painted or antique chairs, free-standing storage, and rustic, bare floorboards or plain flagstones. Almost everything about these dining-areas feels traditional and in a somewhat country style, even though two of the rooms (opposite) are in fact in central city locations – Antwerp and London.

There is a cosiness and warmth about eating in or adjacent to the kitchen. The traditional style suits pretty, often mismatched china, heirloom linen, old glass, and flowers (note how, opposite, left, the owner, a garden designer, has created a pendant light using bottles filled with flowers). The London kitchen-dining room (opposite, right) includes some masterly, historically inspired painted decoration, while, in Antwerp, the walls are covered with a giant tulip design.

Kitchen-Dining
Traditional

An ancient Burgundian house (opposite, left), once home to the estate manager who ran the large chateau across the courtyard, is furnished with appropriate country furniture, some of which came from Argentina. The image opposite, right, shows a spacious kitchen-diner in a Provençal farmhouse. It has been updated, but the locally made tiles, central preparation-and-storage unit and

antique fruitwood table and chairs combine to create a traditional scene.

Above, a run of work surfaces and simple panelled cupboards divides this kitchen in Tuscany, with its small wooden breakfast table, from the much larger, open-plan dining-room. Where they can be accommodated, such different-sized tables are extremely useful, providing the options of breakfast for two in the kitchen area or larger numbers of people around a much bigger table, where upholstered chairs enable long lunches to be taken in comfort.

Kitchen-Dining
Eclectic

To some people, the word 'eclectic' conjures up chaos. Others, however, adore the often-fascinating assemblage of possessions that owners put together in a single space.

In the dining-area opposite, which is reminiscent of a Russian interior, the shrine-like alcove seating, cushions and tablecloth are covered in traditional Eastern European floral prints – the whole planned with an eye to impact and individual pleasure.

In two eighteenth-century houses, one in London, the other in northern France, the principle of 'mix, but no need to match' evokes memories of the sort of dining experiences or atmosphere that one might have enjoyed as a child. The wonderful east London room, for example (left), could be in the home of a stylish eccentric relative rather than being the creation of an accomplished London interior designer.

Living-Dining
Contemporary

Living-cum-dining-rooms are all about the best use of space. It is not always essential to have a dining-table as a focal point. An arrangement that is easy to move against a wall when not in use allows both the extra floor space and the change in the visual focus effectively to expand the real living-area, shifting the emphasis away from the table. This southern Italian holiday home (opposite, bottom) is a good example: the dining-table is used only in winter, allowing the space at other times to remain open as a link between two staircases; with a comfortable sofa at one end, the portion of the room assigned to living is open but separate. The classic use of such space is to place a dining-table between the work area of the kitchen and the living-space, as is well illustrated (below) in this warehouse conversion in Provence.

Living-Dining
Exotic

Pharaonic-like concrete columns provide a strong sense of monumentality and reveal the industrial nature of this London apartment (opposite) owned by a young South African interior designer. The white circular 'pod' behind the dining-area is an office and storage area, an ingenious design solution. The dining-area is opposite the kitchen, which lies to the right, while ample space is left between the dining- and living-spaces. Vintage furniture and African and contemporary pieces are mixed with restraint; the overall impression is one of character and flair.

In a private South African game lodge (right) there are several indoor and outdoor dining-areas. Here, at the end of a covered terrace, the star lighting, a tiny pebbled stream and the bush close at hand conspire to create a more compelling and beguiling setting than city living can provide. In Morocco, a most exotic dining-room (below) has been built at the base of a Berber-inspired lookout tower. The marble-and-oak dining-table was specially commissioned, and stands on a fossil-stone-and-marble floor laid to a design copied from the Vatican.

Materials

Wood is still the most common and sympathetic material for tables and chairs, with styles ranging from chunky ancient oak to pared-down contemporary models. Wood, in all its colours and grains, works in any setting: for example, the small kitchen table placed in the entrance hall of a grand country house (above) does not look out of place, especially as the chairs are typically 'hall' chairs, usually lined up against a wall to seat waiting visitors.

Opposite, top left, natural oak shelving teams well with similarly coloured oak floors throughout the ground floor and extended kitchen-dining room of a Victorian house in London. The owner–designer chose an interesting modern wooden table, with chairs slip-covered in canvas. In two French houses with open-plan living- and dining-areas (opposite, top right and bottom), light wooden chairs effectively balance the sizes and shapes of the more bulky sofa and leather chairs.

Dining Only
Contemporary

A great deal of conservation and restoration was undertaken in this Brussels town house dating from about 1900 (below); its many rooms are filled with a wonderful mix of vintage furniture, from Liberty to Frank Lloyd Wright, and Oceanic and southern African artworks. The lighting, too, is mostly from the mid-twentieth century. The startling contrast of the white, 1970s Danish dining furniture and an enormous contemporary painting in a period panelled room is dramatic.

In a different version of contemporary style, the dining-room in a new central London house (left) is furnished with modern but period-inspired upholstered chairs, their legs, the table and the wooden floor all coloured a similar deep smoky tone. It is an undeniably modern scheme, but one that is rich in comfort and detail.

Ideally, a dining-room should contain storage for china, glassware and cutlery. Opposite, two contemporary dining-rooms, both in nineteenth-century London houses, include built-in cupboards; in one scheme painted a warm orange, in the other – lit by a roof-light – cool green and white. Both rooms are furnished with modern tables, but in each case the look is very different because of the choice of chairs. The chrome-and-black-leather Marcel Breuer design dates from the 1920s, whereas the wooden chairs are modern. Their grid-like backs subtly echo the blocky design of the cupboards.

Dining Only
Traditional

The dining-rooms right and opposite,
top, are classically styled and furnished,
particularly in an Irish castle, where
huge family portraits fill the painted
walls, and sideboards contain cutlery,
glassware, linen and silver. The room
is not decorated in traditional red or
green, however; the colour and velvet
curtains date back to the 1950s. In her
Suffolk country house (opposite, top),
a London-based designer chose
an eighteenth-century-style de Gournay
wallpaper, specially scaled to suit
the room, and she modernized the
delft-lined fireplace by painting the
mantlepiece white.

The use of an all-white Scandinavian
theme in an English panelled dining-room
(below) creates an authentic northern
look. Meanwhile, in a modern London
apartment, window shutters, a Victorian
scrubbed table and Regency chairs,
along with old school radiators and table
lamps, combine to produce a simple but
traditional room.

Dining Only
Conservatory

A shell-encrusted, jewel-box dining-room was built adjacent to the kitchen at the rear of a late seventeenth-century house in London. This was a new construction at basement and ground level, and the owner commissioned a craftsman to create the ambience of a Regency shell grotto. A 1930s stone table is teamed with silver-painted Lloyd Loom chairs, and in candlelight this room is one of the most enchanting dining-rooms imaginable.

In northern Europe's unreliable climate, a glass-walled garden room in Antwerp is used for dining, reading, painting and relaxing (opposite, top). In Provence, however, shade is more important than shelter, and by using only glass at one end of the room (opposite, bottom), the owner–designer was able to preserve the extraordinary views of her farm and the hills beyond. The room is so light that potted plants thrive amid the dappled sunlight.

Dining Only
Colour

The German owner–designer of this glittering room (opposite) has taken the aubergine hall colour through to his dining-room and chosen silk curtains of the same colour. This is a modern rather than traditional shade, but the selection of furniture, lamps, carpet and pictures defies a specific dateline. The reflective surface of the table, very much designed for evening entertaining by candlelight, enhances the crystal candelabra and ensures that the focus of the evening is upon the guests.

Again, below, the orange-coral-coloured walls are somewhat unusual in an English country house, but the hand-painted gold tree with tiny birds appearing to alight is in the tradition of period wallpaper decoration. This is a warm and welcoming colour scheme, flattering and glowing by firelight. The large number of leather-bound books displayed in the room complements the overall scheme extremely well.

Contemporary Lighting

It has never been easier to provide just the right amount of light above a dining-room table. Ceiling-mounted downlights are not the solution, but in recent years manufacturers have realized that two types of lighting in particular were in great demand. Industrial-looking chrome and aluminium, and simple pendants with oversized shades, either painted metal or fabric – great, elongated boxes of transparent linen or silk – set the trend. Because the light is diffused and directed by the shade, diners are not sitting under spotlights. The elegant breakfast-dining-room (right) features, between the windows, stainless-steel surface-mounted up- and downlights with adjustable beam widths. Above the table is a glazed roof-light, in the centre of which is a white linen pendant fitting by Giorgetti of Italy.

Candles and Crystal Lights

Light by which to dine is really the only non-task lighting in a house, so a low-wattage feature light above the table is often sufficient, although a couple of silver, porcelain or crystal candelabra placed on the table add to the intimate atmosphere.

Fire hazards aside, it really does not matter how candles are used to light a dining-area (although many are better than few): candlelight is the most intimate and cosy of all. Traditional crystal chandeliers, unwired and with holders for eight or ten candles, provide a sort of crowning glory to a beautifully laid table, but modern versions are equally attractive. Below, right, the two simple iron circles hung in the dining-room of a house in Menerbes, in the South of France, break up the straight lines of the table, antique cupboard and ceiling space. Meanwhile, in a very differently styled interior (below, left), the delicate mixture of orchids and candles on the table echoes the pattern on the screen behind. The suspended 'shelf' in a more modern space (far right) imitates the linen-box fitting that has become so popular.

Contemporary Furniture

Verner Panton's stacking chair of 1959 was the first single-material, single-form injection-moulded chair. The black chairs seen here in a Modernist home outside Marrakesh were made in Morocco, probably in the 1960s; this very popular model was reissued by Vitra in 1990.

Modern dining-areas often feature a most interesting mix of materials and styles. Why place wooden chairs necessarily with a matching wooden table? The 1970s chairs and trestle table in an ancient stone chateau kitchen-dining room (right) work perfectly; it is a younger, fresher approach, where in the past rustic oak might have been deemed more appropriate. A group of sinuous Frank Gehry plywood chairs (opposite, bottom left) is teamed with a dark Modenature table. In a London designer's apartment near Tower Bridge, Philippe Starck black leather-and-steel chairs from the 1980s, a Rosso Verona marble-topped table on a black base, a gilt lamp and a coral-inspired frame make a witty and educated grouping; near by stands a second table, this one by Matthew Hilton.

Upholstered Chairs

While not all wood, wire or moulded chairs are uncomfortable, there is nothing quite like the pleasures of truly comfortable dining-room seating. The style is not important, but the width and depth of the seat and the angle of the back of a chair are crucial considerations.

Leather upholstery, in myriad colours and fine finishes, is the practical and luxurious choice for three homes shown here. The Spanish designer who refurbished and furnished a villa near Marbella (opposite, left) buys specific design names, such as Fendi, Casa Armani and John Hutton, citing comfort and proportion as paramount. The close-nailed, slightly wing-backed chairs seen opposite, right, appear to wrap, cosseting and secure, around the dining-table. Note that all the chairs illustrated have unadorned, dark-coloured legs; modern chairs do not require fussy, complicated support.

Miscellaneous Chairs

Shiny aluminium chairs in their many guises are light, easy to move about and successfully double as extra seating in any room in the house; they are a sort of go-anywhere chair. The combination of an old kitchen table with modern chairs, pretty crystal candelabra and a lime-yellow wall colour creates a fresh and exciting look.

By placing two gigantic, simply framed mirrors at either end of a long, narrow dining-room, the owners of this Marrakesh house (opposite, left) effectively doubled the sense of space. Numerous bentwood-style chairs, probably from a hotel or restaurant refurbishment, were found in the local flea market, as was the orange velvet to make the loose seat covers.

Cane chairs suit warm climates. In a suite of rooms of magnificent proportions in a South African game lodge, the feeling is summery; a glass-topped trestle table and a centrally placed glass pendant light, together with plenty of silver candlesticks, form a sophisticated but definitely relaxed dining experience.

Cupboards and Dressers

All the cupboards and chests and one of the tables shown here are made of wood, some pieces painted, others showing off the extraordinary grains and patterns that so many woods display when cut and polished. The differing styles are intriguing, from a 'palazzo'-style Italian piece dating from the 1940s, with mirrored insets (left), to the beautifully textured Karl Hahn chest with stone handles, dating from the 1970s, its surface created by burning and sandblasting.

The convincing console in a French house dating from about 1800 (below, right) is one of a pair made and painted by the owner, an English interior designer. Large painted dressers and chests are typical examples of dining storage in Provençal houses, and are often painted in mellow tones of grey, green, blue and off-white. In dining-rooms where linen tablecloths and napkins are used regularly, a chest of drawers is the best way to keep those starched and precious items to hand.

Working

The communications revolution of the last few decades has led to 'homework' acquiring an entirely new meaning. As working from home, either full or part time, becomes more prevalent across the globe, more and more ways of accommodating the means – from a single wireless laptop to a sophisticated communications centre – are found within homes of greatly differing sizes and styles. While one may mourn the fact that the gentle art of letter-writing at a specially made desk in a quiet corner has suffered a sad decline (good-sized heirloom writing-tables and desks survive, but the extraordinarily tiny and dainty ladies' 'bureaux' of yesteryear are increasingly rare), at the same time one can admire people who have achieved a virtually paper-free life, and envy those with enough space to dedicate a whole room to work.

Whatever the space, good design and/or careful storage are paramount to working successfully from home. Sleek, discreet workstations, as opposed to massive, purpose-made desks, can now be seen fitted into all manner of niches in almost any room of a house or apartment. Children use computers from a young age and often have a study area incorporated into their bedrooms. Many families have a communal work space in the kitchen or slotted neatly under a staircase. Where space is at a premium, a landing may be ideal for use as a study, since many boast a large window and are square, enabling two walls to be fitted out with worktops, shelving and cupboards. Where no dedicated space can be created, the kitchen or dining-table remains, as always, a valuable last resort.

Contemporary

Inevitably, the type of work carried out in a home is a key factor in deciding how much space to allocate to it. Although the height of working luxury is surely a room with a view, good natural light and miles of work surfaces and storage space (opposite, top), a multi-tasking space can nonetheless be more sociable and equally efficient. Opposite, bottom, a garden extension to a terraced house in central

London is furnished for family use. Games, seating and plenty of work space ensure that this light and airy room functions equally well for adults and children.

Contemporary working spaces tend to feature clean lines and clear work surfaces, and are designed so that the paraphernalia of work is largely hidden in cupboards or drawers. What little is on display is either purely practical in nature – a computer screen, a lamp

and a telephone – or may include just one or two favourite objects, such as a box for stamps and an interesting clock or sculpture. In this dressing-room with an integrated work desk (above), rigorous attention to detail was paid to the design and finish. The walls, cupboards and desk were specially made in grey-dyed sycamore with stainless-steel banding. There is, however, no indication of what kind of work takes place.

Contemporary

Three very different styles are illustrated here. Opposite, a wall of bookshelves and a deep sofa apparently indicate less work and more leisure; nonetheless, since reading can be such an important part of work, the creation of such a relaxing, calm environment is ideal. Here, the sense of tranquillity is intensified by restricting strong colours to the shelving and the books themselves.

The teenage bedroom-cum-study-cum-sitting-room (above) is a good example of how to use space to its fullest potential, where each area is clearly but subtly delineated through the use of blinds, curtains and a rug. In the third example (right), the choice of a trestle table and shelving in matching, pale-toned wood reveals that the owner has thought about how the furniture will harmonize. A pair of lamps with a painted sign hung in between creates a pleasing symmetry and focal point.

Traditional

In this context, 'traditional' refers purely to the choice of furnishings and decoration in a room where part or all of the available space is used for work activity. In each case there is some antique furniture, but none of the rooms is entirely what might be called an 'office'. For example, the room featuring the very large table (opposite, bottom left) can be used for dining, although the house also contains a dining-room; this room is treated as a transition between it and the living-room beyond. On the table, large books can be displayed and browsed, plans laid out, or photographs studied; it is a luxury space with innumerable uses.

In the days when guests were expected to spend time alone between meals and entertainment, bedrooms in larger houses traditionally contained a writing-table or desk, the owner supplying stationery and stamps. Three variations on this theme are shown here, deploying differing degrees of formality. To the right, the size and busyness of the desk show clearly that its owner centres a significant part of his life here.

Finally, a private nook in the corner of a well-equipped home office in east London (opposite, top left), with a comfortable chair and a round table placed thoughtfully by the window and bearing a stack of books, invites the owner or any visitor to sit down and enjoy a quiet read. The wall of storage cupboards was designed to be in keeping with the rest of the house, which features fine paint effects and much custom-made furniture, cabinetry and lighting.

Tables, Desks and Chairs

Furniture designed for work can be a powerful statement of taste, and may be designed specifically to fit into a particular room scheme. Here, a pair of vintage barstools is placed beside a slim, polished-plaster counter in a Marrakesh riad. In such a narrow room, this is an efficient, if a little restricted, way to house files and provide a writing-surface from which to despatch domestic business. In contrast, opposite, top left, a first-floor landing is treated as a more serious home office, its imposing walnut desk, capacious chair and packed shelves highlighting that this is a study where reference books are frequently used. Elsewhere (opposite, bottom left), a well-made old-fashioned desk, chair and drawer unit chime perfectly with the period panelled rooms of an older house, and provide an effective and focused place in which to work free from distraction.

Where swivel chairs – whether modern or antique – on wheels are employed, a bare floor surface is more practical than carpet. Although some writers swear by the use of a hard chair, for other workers, the comfort of the seating is crucial to their achieving a good day's work. In all cases, good task lighting is a must.

Otherwise, the decoration of work areas is as varied as the choice of furniture, and depends very much on the individual's need to be either shielded from or bolstered and inspired by potential diversions. In the same way that various criteria come into play in the decor of a kitchen, there are people who thrive surrounded by the clutter of magazines, books, pictures and photographs, while others require nothing but a laptop, a pen and a block of paper.

Tables, Desks and Chairs

Provided it is firm and even, a work surface can be made of almost anything. Here we see velvety smooth white Corian in a contemporary house in southern Spain; a glass-topped vintage writing-desk; and a fine Italian design (below, left and right) in Macassar ebony by Giorgetti (the lamp is by Romeo Sozzi from Promemoria). All are very different in both style and material, but equally pleasing and efficient. Seating varies greatly, too. Where the user may spend all day at a table, a comfortable chair, such as the leather one by Giorgetti (below, right) is essential. By contrast, occasional work, such as that done at this meeting-table in a dress-designer's studio (opposite, top left), does not require ergonomically designed chairs. Rather, style, as much as comfort, can dictate the choice.

Shelving

Social and technological change have blurred the boundaries between home libraries, which contained books kept for pleasure, and the inevitable combination of files, folios, CD-ROMs, other reference material and books that is now frequently used in a home office. In spite of the technological revolution, many home workers – whether architects or barristers, chefs or shipping agents – find that the internet does not always deliver the sort of satisfying wealth of information provided by a collection of old and new books. Computer-generated material may not be as accurate, and it cannot create the magical and irresistible ambience produced by shelves of reference books, their colours, typefaces, sizes and shapes all contributing tangibly to our sense of the power of knowledge. Although there are regular dire predictions about the demise of books, almost nobody feels at home without them, even if the books are entirely work-related in subject-matter.

The storage of all manner of printed information is of course about personal choice, although accessibility is a key consideration. Open or enclosed storage are the two options. Shelves continue to be the practical, most versatile and stimulating choice, but in the most contemporary interiors, even shelves are likely to be hidden behind doors.

By contrast, in an attic conversion in a Hamburg villa, a dramatic book tower (opposite, left), which disguises the lift access, has open shelves. Files and frequently used books are stored on the lower levels, and reference books above.

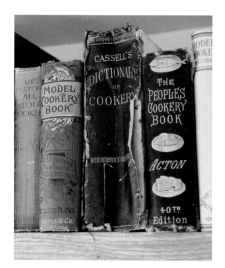

Inspiration

The particular demands of different types of work are so diverse, as are the ways in which we enable ourselves to fulfil them, that in the styling or design of a private homework space, it is true that anything goes if it works for the person who creates it. Here we see how working from home frees people to express their individuality. For example, the intriguing creatures on sticks (opposite, bottom right) were made by Dutch artist Berend Hoekstra for a working home library in central Brussels: no matter how well one catalogues groups of books, a marker to indicate which titles are relevant to one's current research is always useful.

Inevitably, collectors often work among their prized possessions: illustrated below is the study of a man who works surrounded by a trove of Oceanic and southern African art. Antiques dealers may choose furniture from their stock, creating highly individual rooms by using rare or unique objects, and perhaps parting with pieces every few months or so and replacing them with others that have caught their fancy. Likewise, designers frequently decorate their own work area in a much quirkier way than they might for a client.

Bedrooms

There was a time, hard to imagine now, when the bedrooms of the wealthy were furnished and decorated for entertaining, the owner reclining in great style upon a dais-mounted bed. Sumptuous velvets, embroidery and silks were employed in the manner of a salon, and the bed itself was the most expensive article of furniture in the house. It was partly the introduction of cotton and linen fabrics into the bedroom (replacing wool and silk), along with the realization that light and fresh air were not unhealthy, that brought about a change in decoration. Old household records show that before chintz became readily available, white linen curtains were used for both beds and windows.

Today's bedrooms continue to reflect many centuries of history, including the fact that a top-of-the-range bed can still be our most expensive acquisition. Bedrooms are now the most private of rooms, but the unequivocal need for sleep in the most comfortable bed possible never changes. Four-poster beds are popular in all their guises; bed curtains of all sorts, no longer required for warmth or privacy, but purely for decorative pleasure, continue to provide a comforting sense of enclosure. While modern beds are generally much plainer – mere platforms for sleeping – linen, pillows and lighting are carefully selected to achieve a specific look. There is much talk about a bedroom needing to be a calm, personal retreat, but as we shall see in this chapter, not everyone agrees that calm is simply created by neutral decoration, pale colour schemes and simplicity.

Contemporary
Monochrome

'Monochrome' is, strictly, a black-and white image, or a room containing only variations of a single colour. Here, however, the term is used to describe bedrooms where the owners have deliberately chosen to avoid any mixture of colours beyond those of wood, leather and tonal fabric. These calm and uncluttered rooms are far from sterile. In each case a degree of comfort and practicality is considered – a chair to relax in, and perhaps separate storage facilities outside the bedroom itself. The style is quiet, even peaceful. From almost entirely white to a room that is furnished and decorated in dark browns partnered with a paler taupe and stone, the impression overall is of a single composition, even though each room is wholly different in style.

Despite the neutrality of the colours, the effect need not be bland: for example, the owner of a Brussels town house (below, right) has placed a rare and exquisite eighteenth-century Japanese silver screen alongside a Baining tapa piece and a vintage metal chair to create a unique and striking decor.

Contemporary
Monochrome

These bedrooms are decorated and furnished with more than just the room itself in mind. A wall of steel panelling (right) was designed as part of the complete refurbishment of a London warehouse apartment, in which industrial elements of the past were reinterpreted throughout. Although the walls in the room below are lined with fabric, the colour is hard to define; combined with off-white linen, pale floors and a quality steel fire surround, the look becomes almost colourless.

Pure-white bed linen stands in clear contrast to other neutrals, but in the Moroccan bedroom opposite, bottom, a traditional timber ceiling, an adobe wall finish, a palm-trunk construction (whole palm trunks were used as pillars in the opening between the bedroom and the dressing-room) and an old farm door, as well as the hand-woven Berber blanket on the bed, all blend into a satisfying organic colour scheme, which is repeated throughout the house.

Even modern monochrome requires some contrast, which is well illustrated in a London bedroom (opposite, top). While the floors, walls, bed and pillows are of very similar tones, the dark side tables and ivory lampshades relieve any sense of blandness.

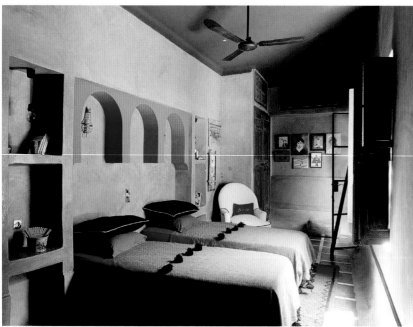

Contemporary
Eclectic

Although undeniably modern, each of these rooms possesses a particularly individual appearance, created partly by its location as well as by the choice of contents and decoration. The two bedrooms shown opposite, top, both situated in a Madrid mansion block, rely on large-scale works of art and an unusual mix of furniture and lighting to add interest to the neutral decoration. The owner of a twin-bedded guest room in Marrakesh (opposite, bottom left) has taken an architectural motif for a raised headboard that links the beds by colour and by creating a bridge-like span between the storage units on either side.

The rooms in Moroccan courtyard houses are usually very narrow. By building a partial wall with a spot-lit niche behind the bed (opposite, bottom right), a bathroom, accessed from both sides, is neatly fitted into the long, narrow space; the whole is treated to a cool-grey plaster finish. An altogether grander scheme (right) by a London interior designer features a coved ceiling, mirror panels, fabric-covered cupboards and a bed that appears to float above a recessed platform. Quite masculine in style, this look depends upon fine-quality materials and the best craftsmanship.

Tradition and Comfort
Country

People choose what is called 'country style' for differing reasons: perhaps – most naturally, but not exclusively – because they own a country house, or because the architecture of a property lends itself to the style. Country-style decoration is international and, in its appeal, the most enduring of all. It is unstructured, and favours craftsmanship over mass production.

The complex timbers in a French chateau create a strong background for this bedroom (below), which is furnished with a pair of metal beds, a vintage table and leather chairs. A very different country look has been created by using an all-white colour scheme and furniture of similar provenance (right), an altogether Scandinavian rather than English look. Opposite, top and bottom, curtained, decorative iron beds; exposed wall structures; the choice of an elegant but rustic sofa; and an iron cafe table are all hallmarks of a refined version of the country style.

Tradition and Comfort
Colour

Traditional national or regional colour schemes often determine the way in which interiors are decorated, particularly in countries where certain wall and floor finishes are common or vernacular. The two Moroccan bedrooms seen here (left, and opposite, bottom) are both in a riad in Marrakesh and feature polished-plaster walls. The first is coloured pale grey and the second an earth-toned ochre, a colour of many hues that is found all over the city, from the ancient defensive walls to newly built villas; it is a warm tone without being a hot colour. Although the house has undergone major restoration, the English owner was keen to retain traditional elements wherever possible; the blue corner fireplace, for example, provides a quaint and striking focal point as well as warmth in the winter. Both beds have locally made striped covers, each picking up the various tones of the rooms.

In Spain, in a large, rambling old house north of Cadiz, the floor tiles in a guest bedroom determined the stippled pink wall colour, which produces a soft, dreamy background to an old rug, damask curtains and a crackled oil painting, combined with modern bedside tables and lamps.

Tradition and Comfort
Bedheads

Bedheads, whether upholstered or not, are constantly changing in style, and always have done. High or low, brass-railed or solid wood, traditional beds vary greatly from country to country and even by region. In a room that is quite traditionally furnished with an elegant wing-back chair and bedside chests of drawers (below, right), the bedhead is a modern, buttoned and upholstered creation, and anchors the bed in a room that lacks strict symmetry. The painted French bed (right) in a guest room in an English country house has been treated to silk upholstery at head and foot, an eiderdown – that most traditional of covers – and a French-style hanging.

Old beds were much higher than modern styles tend to be; the brass bed shown below, in a French country house, relies on large pillows to support reclining and reading, and thereby gives the impression of great comfort.

Tradition and Comfort
Four-Posters

A fine antique four-poster bed, canopied, curtained and draped with heirloom linen and lace, is a sight to behold. Many traditionally decorated bedrooms are based on a nineteenth-century style, where – although the houses of the well-to-do were usually large – the bedroom was treated as a personal space for reading and writing as well as for sleeping. Floral-patterned wallpaper and curtains, close-hung watercolours, wardrobes, chairs and chests – there was a lot going on.

On either side of a gloriously old-fashioned room (above, left) are images showing two French country bedrooms. One feels 'colonial', with a teak bed, dark furniture and woven baskets used for storage and as tabletops. It is clear that the owners spend time in Africa, and although the contents are modern, the ensemble nonetheless has a definite feel of the past about it. By contrast, in the bedroom shown above, right, an antique painted chest, oriental carpet and traditional *boutis* quilt add period glamour to this very pretty and charming country scheme.

Lighting
Principles

Lighting design has come a long way in recent years. The choice is greater than ever, but when it comes to bedrooms, great banks of ceiling-mounted downlights are not appropriate; the same goes for recessed, strip or spotlights and LEDs. Table lamps, placed on chests or bedside tables for specific tasks – reading, for example, or finding one's way about the room – are ideal. Floor lights are less common in bedrooms, but are worth consideration, as they provide valuable additional light in corners, or can usefully fill a space too small for furniture.

Lamp bases can be made of just about anything – glass, crystal, metal, marble, wood and candlesticks – although classic columns, urns and slender glass shapes are perennial favourites. A growing number of interior designers commission specially made lamps in various sizes; as the style, shape and colour of shades are important considerations, these, too, are often customized for each lamp and room.

Lighting
Contemporary

The perfectly named *Icarus* light, mimicking the tail feathers of a white peacock, appears to hover above the bed in this London house. Pendant lighting is less about practicality and more about beauty, but it is also an effective way to break up expanses of white ceiling or demarcate different living-areas. A pair of stunning 1920s coloured Murano glass lamps, topped with simple, white card shades and set on modern lacquered side tables, are just the right height for reading. Twentieth-century chrome desk lamps (opposite, right) are the most practical of all bedroom lights, since they can be adjusted at two points. Their classic design works equally well in a traditional or a contemporary scheme.

Lighting
Contemporary

In a lovely old house in Antwerp (opposite), the bedroom, painted dark blue and adorned with printed linen curtains, is a traditionally decorated room but for the bedside lights. Inconspicuous but entirely practical, these floor lamps with tiny lily-shaped shades are a great choice for a reading-light in a room otherwise furnished with antiques. Floor lamps, as we have seen (pages 224–25), provide higher-level lighting than their bedside counterparts, and are particularly useful in large rooms, especially for focusing on a seating area – as here (far right), beside a pair of *Barcelona* white leather chairs placed in the centre of the room – or for illuminating dark nooks.

In new and refurbished homes, electric sockets can be placed in the floors and walls according to a pre-designed furniture plan, thereby affording greater flexibility for lighting. The four bedrooms on the right, in houses of greatly differing ages and styles, are variously located in London, France, Germany and Spain, but each one features modern lamp designs.

Lighting
Glass and Decorative

Decorative lighting need not necessarily hark back to old times, although the use of period lighting in a room otherwise furnished and decorated in an entirely modern style is an enduring trend. Chandeliers were once found only in ballrooms, dining-rooms or drawing-rooms, but for a decade or more now, owners and designers have been inspired to use French, English, Italian or Bohemian gilt and crystal, Murano glass or contemporary Perspex designs in virtually every room in a house. A crystal chandelier, polished and glittering beneath numerous bulbs, is always a romantic addition to a bedroom, whether contemporary or traditional. The chandeliers shown here are in English homes, while the teardrop glass lamp on a beautifully figured chest of drawers (far right) is in the Italian holiday home of an English interior designer; in the guest room of the same house (below, left) is an unusual 'storm lantern'.

A tiny brass lamp with tendrils and cut-crystal drops (opposite, top right) is typically French, while marble or alabaster urns continue to have universal appeal. Candles – impractical, yet beguiling – provide minimum light but maximum ambience.

Fabrics and Patterns
Curtains

The choice of fabric for curtains and upholstery is vast; the decision about which fabric to choose will be influenced partly by climate and light, and partly by the amount of decorative impact that is required from curtains, chairs or sofas. Obviously, the less colour and pattern are involved, the quieter the overall look will be. In a French house with window

shutters (above, left), the curtains do not need to block out light, and although these filmy stripes can be drawn, they serve principally to frame the window and create a link to the blue-and-white cotton toile upholstery on a pair of chairs and footstools.

The owner of a large house in Marrakesh chose simple white calico for all the curtains in the house and, in dramatic contrast, richly coloured plain velvet for the upholstery. In a guest bedroom (opposite, right), a London

interior designer has layered two sets of curtains. The sheer, vertical stripe in red and orange creates a summery look for the room during the day, while a pair of handmade, lined curtains with a tiny fringed leading edge block out unwanted early-morning sun and are cosy in winter.

Fabrics and Patterns
Materials and Carpets

Animal-hide floor coverings – nowadays often printed or woven rather than the real thing – have been used for centuries, although it was probably the iconic white bedroom that Nancy Lancaster designed at her eighteenth-century home, Kelmarsh Hall, featuring a zebra-hide rug, that inspired the enduring popularity of the zebra pattern. Recently, cowhides have also become popular. A London interior designer and antiques dealer likes sheep- and goatskin rugs (left). In her daughter's bedroom, she has used quantities of red velvet to curtain a wardrobe and casually to dress up an old sofa: the look is soft and luxurious.

In a London warehouse conversion, in a room lined in figured timber panelling, green velvet was used to upholster a bedroom chair, to provide a pleasing contrast and texture. Opposite, bottom, the Spanish designer of a villa and guest house chose bedroom furniture from Fendi, with the large bedhead upholstered in gold-toned silk velvet. The bedcovers and wall colouring are on a similar spectrum, but in more earthy tones. In her London apartment, a young antiques dealer has draped an old embroidered silk shawl over the balustrade of her mezzanine bedroom, for the pleasure of seeing a work of art and to provide a little privacy.

Fabrics and Patterns
Wallpaper

Wallpaper was never as favoured in Europe, apart from France, as in Britain and the United States. Fine examples of eighteenth- and nineteenth-century hand-painted chinoiserie papers can be seen in a number of houses belonging to the National Trust in Britain. Wallpaper – both the archive document designs seen opposite, left, and opposite, bottom right, and modern interpretations that are often over-scaled floral designs of only two colours – is as popular as ever. In the images right and below, only one wall has been papered, whereas traditionally the whole room would have been covered; in the French way, the ceiling would also have been papered, as it has been here (opposite, left) in an Irish castle.

Trends in wallpaper are constantly changing – gold and silver leaf are currently in vogue – and the traditional manufacturers have kept pace, regularly reworking colourways and the scale of patterns. As these images show, wallpaper creates a more cosseting and softer environment than paint, and will remain a favoured choice for bedroom decoration, where its patterns can be appreciated at leisure. Indeed, in a child's bedroom, such patterns may come to form one of the sleeper's earliest memories.

Fabrics and Patterns
Bright Colours

Children love bright colours and enjoy choosing the decoration for their own bedrooms, sometimes with exciting results. The orange-and-yellow scheme above is fun, mixing in lilac, pink, blue and beige: it is young but not at all childish. Multicoloured striped bedcovers in printed linen or woven wool are a simple means of livening up a large expanse of bed, especially in a room with little other colour or decoration, as are patchwork quilts (opposite, top right). Wonderfully old-fashioned and still popular, they are a great way to use up scraps of old fabric, and bring a burst of colour to a bedroom.

In a romantic attic guest bedroom in a French village house (opposite, left), where the walls are painted a warm pink and the floor is covered with a delicate needlepoint rug, a rich-pink velvet chaise longue adds a vibrant dash of colour.

Fabrics and Patterns
Bed Hangings

There is nothing quite as luxurious as a fully canopied four-poster bed or an elaborate half-tester created from many metres of one's favourite fabric. An exotic ensemble has been created by a couturier in London (opposite, bottom left); his bedroom walls are lined in felt with a lace border, and the bed is adorned with layers of fabrics, Turkish embroidery and fine bedlinen, the whole topped off with regal feathers. The room is also crammed with unusual objects.

In a Provençal country house, a single white-and-red, subtly striped linen was chosen for the canopy, curtains, valance, bedcover and headboard; a similar, rustier-red blanket and upholstered stool link well to the terracotta-tiled floors. In northern France, the master bedroom in a village house (opposite, bottom right) is dressed with antique bedlinen, a pretty white corona and curtains.

An English interior designer used plain silks to dress up her country-house bed (above, right); meanwhile, in southern Italy (above, left), simple muslin hangings, attached to a painted modern bed-frame, are diaphanous and airy, perfect in a hot climate. Plain white hangings, along with a traditional printed quilt, also set off a bed with barley-sugar wooden posts (opposite, top left) and its matching side table; with such elaborately carved furniture, more patterns would be confusing.

Fabrics and Patterns
Details

Fabric is a key and versatile element in decoration, and the bedroom is a highly appropriate space in which to make the most of its potential: not only does a bedroom need a fair amount of fabric for bedcovers, curtains and furniture, but it is also a place where the occupant might have time to appreciate the selected scheme. Plain or patterned,

floral or geometric, stripes and checks, spots, dots or embroidered designs – the possibilities for mixing, matching and co-ordinating are always exciting. Fashion may play a large part in dictating the choice, but there are popular and enduring styles, such as the blue-and-ivory toile-de-Jouy print seen here, stylishly lined with a cotton printed in tiny checks and hung from a painted corona.

Quilted bedcovers made from cotton, linen or silk provide a tidy finish to the layers of bedding beneath. Multiple

down-filled pillows of differing sizes, some for sleep, others for decoration, can be covered in printed fabric or embroidered to order: the stitched fine linen seen above was supplied by the Monogrammed Linen Shop in London. A four-poster bed in an Irish castle has been treated to a classic tightly pleated fabric canopy finished with a rosette. In a bedroom in France (opposite, bottom right), white linen hangings are attached to wooden railings by simple, biscuit-coloured headings.

Classic Beds

Much of what we term 'classic' decoration, furnishing and use of fabrics originated in France. The beds and daybed seen here, all of which are influenced by French style, derive their design from the eighteenth century. Only one, however – the daybed, smartly upholstered in taupe-coloured linen – is in France, in a newly restored house in Provence. The panelled room is in east London, while the alcove and white-painted beds (below, left, and opposite) are in Germany. In the London room (right), oyster-grey silk has been used for the bedcover and bolsters, and the furniture has been placed in such a way as to re-create a historic tableau convincingly. What each room has in common is a timelessness; there is little clue as to whether the beds and decoration, or the fabrics and furniture, were chosen recently or not.

Simple Four-Poster Beds

Unadorned, and of different styles, each of these four-poster beds makes a sculptural impact in a bedroom – in particular, creating vertical interest where the ceilings are low. The small painted bed (above) was brought back by its owner from a former home in Brazil. A soaring beamed ceiling in a Provençal house sets off a modern white bed, although the fabric used for the headboard is in a traditional print.

Furnishing a large French chateau, the owner bought beds, chests and cupboards directly from the Far East, the styles and colour of the furniture being eminently well suited to the very large rooms (opposite, top right). By contrast, the unusual curved wooden headboard design with open-work posts (opposite, top left) graces an English country house.

Brass beds of differing styles have long been a favourite in many countries: the bed seen here (opposite, bottom left) is in a Spanish house.

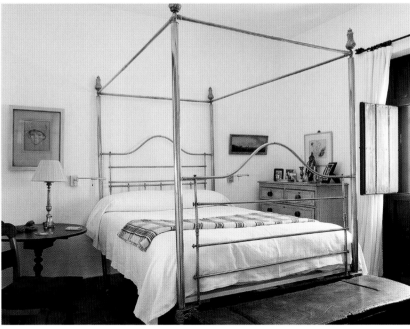

Children's Beds

Two very contrasting children's bedrooms are illustrated here. With a nod to the past, the young girl's room in a central London house is painted in complementary tones of pale lilac and lime green; a printed border has been used to separate the colours. The *lit-bateau* bed is dressed with a mosquito net, whimsical and pretty rather than essential. Cream wool carpet makes this room a cosy and comfortable play space, albeit one in which no drinks or food can practically be allowed. What fun children must have in raised, tent-like beds with windows (opposite), where the space beneath is an ideal play area roofed, as it were, by the beds themselves.

Custom Cabinetry

No matter how hard we try to simplify our lives, the need and desire for good storage facilities remain universal, particularly where clothes, shoes, bags and belts are concerned. Designers and clients are increasingly prepared to allocate considerable space – often an adjoining spare bedroom – for conversion into meticulously planned storage spaces.

What these images have in common is high-quality cabinetry, much like shop fittings and indeed, in some cases, made by professional shop fitters. Where space allows, an 'island' unit (opposite) is ideal for laying out an outfit and matching accessories; it is so much better than having to use the bed.

Even where a full dressing-room is not possible, halls and corridors can be lined with slim shelving or cupboards. Particular attention should be paid to lighting: angled spotlights are ideal to provide task lighting for specific areas. Note how above, right, drawers have been included along with open shelves and hanging space.

Shelving and drawers do not need to be deep to store folded garments, bags or shoes, which ideally it should be possible to see and access with ease. Such well-designed storage alleviates both chaos and creases.

Drawers

A streamlined Alpi-veneered, rise-and-fall television unit was specially created by the designer of a glamorous London home. The gently curved opening ends and horizontal lines – finger grooves, which enable the piece to open without the need for handles – make this a most elegant piece of contemporary furniture, which teams well with a Donghia *Shell* chair and gold-dusted floor lamp.

A pair of tall, narrow, mirror-panelled chests is set between the bedroom windows in a French seaside holiday home (below, left), while in a Spanish house an ebonized chest of drawers works well in combination with the black metal bed and curtain rails and the dark picture and frame. In an English dressing-room (opposite, top), a limed-oak cabinet by Heals & Son has useful slim drawers and a pull-out surface.

An impressive vintage steel cabinet (opposite, bottom left) is placed against an equally industrial-looking wall finish in a converted warehouse. On a more traditional note, a collector found an unusually large, antique Japanese Tansu kitchen cupboard-and-drawer unit for his bedroom. Fittingly, he has topped it with a collection of patinated-bronze Japanese pots.

Wardrobes

Whether installed in a separate dressing-room or in a bedroom large enough to contain a wall of cupboards, built-in storage is more efficient and capable of containing larger amounts of clothing and possessions than the free-standing armoires and wardrobes of yesteryear.

In two London bedrooms shown here (right, and opposite, top left), fabric has been used to cover the cupboard doors. Soft and tactile, fabric is ideal in a room that is not subject to heavy wear and tear. A dress-designer's bedroom is furnished with white painted cupboards with pretty applied mouldings, and she makes good use of the space above to stack storage boxes. In the south of France, lattice doors allow air to circulate, while in Antwerp, oak was used to fit out a dressing-area off the master bedroom. When cupboards extend to ceiling height, they tend – somewhat paradoxically – to diminish visually, creating less impact in a room.

Children's Storage

Bedroom storage for young children is less about lots of clothes, and more about their toys and books. Children's bedrooms are often places to play as well as to sleep. The circular unit in a French chateau was designed as a 'pod' in the centre of a large room for two young boys, leaving the bedroom itself uncluttered by cupboards or wardrobes.

Older children, especially girls, often want bright colours, but in these modern rooms for younger offspring, it is interesting that the parents have mostly used white paint, fabric and rugs as a good foil for the toys and books, which are colourful enough. An old French armoire, the most traditional of storage units, appears bright and fresh after a coat of white paint and the removal of its door panels (opposite, bottom left); by contrast, the wire units (opposite, top left) are the most contemporary of storage solutions. It is worth noting that each of these pieces of furniture allows all the owners' possessions to be seen and easily found.

Fancy Dressing-Tables

A lace-skirted dressing-table with pretty pleated-fabric lampshades, a curvaceous mirror and a comfortable upholstered stool is perhaps the most English and timeless of bedroom scenes. Traditionally, women sat before a mirror, created a hairstyle, applied their make-up and powdered their noses – a relaxing ritual that has almost disappeared as the focus has shifted to speed and large, well-equipped bathrooms. Nevertheless, the dressing-table, or chest, remains a key element in most women's bedrooms. It is a very personal piece of furniture: small drawers, as shown here, are ideal for storing costume jewellery, hair clips, scent and all the little intimate things one collects over the years.

Wooden Dressing-Tables

The tables and chests seen here – mahogany, pine and faux-bamboo, each of different styles and dates – are all useful additions in bedrooms where dressing, or even perhaps just a glance in a mirror, takes place. Opposite, left, is a tiny writing-desk, topped with an old-fashioned jug and bowl, evoking nostalgia for a time when these items were in daily use. In a Suffolk country house a set of ivory-backed brushes, possibly still in use, is displayed on a fine chest with an elegant dressing-mirror to match.

The owner of a Sussex house has arranged favourite woven baskets, a fan and an oval hand-mirror on a nineteenth-century chest of drawers: cosmetics and scent bottles tend to be stored in bathrooms now, while bedroom surfaces are typically used to show things one simply likes to look at or have close by.

Miscellaneous Furniture

Ideally, every bedroom should contain at least one interesting chair or a sofa and, where space permits, a table for books and flowers. A Perspex *Louis Ghost* chair by Philippe Starck has been adorned with tassels that soften its outline and well suit its placement in a summery white bedroom in the South of France. The neat little 1930s sofa, upholstered in a grey chenille fabric with plump silk cushions, is a smart addition to a country bedroom where the colour scheme ranges through cream and grey tones.

Vintage furniture in particular, and certain antiques, can be attractive elements in otherwise contemporary interiors. Below, left and right, are two good examples of smart, small and practical vintage bedside tables, each topped with an interesting modern lamp. Many kinds of twentieth-century furniture suit houses and apartments that lack period architectural detail. Period clothing can also be framed and displayed in the bedroom to great effect. Below, right, this child's dress belongs to a Belgian artist and creator of collections of painted paper dresses that have been exhibited all over the world.

Opposite, two London designers have taken very different approaches to bedrooms: through the artful use of interesting objects and very subtle neutrals, one has created a modern 'period' style; the other has used a dark trestle-table, mirror and lamp to make a sculptural, practical and pleasing contemporary grouping.

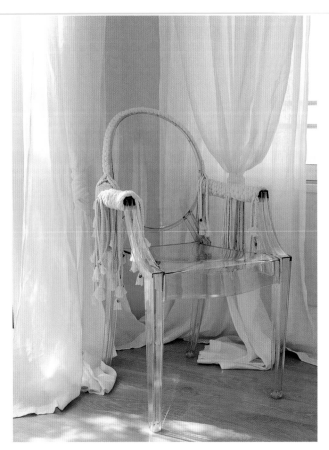

Bathrooms

It may well have been the English designer David Hicks who began the modern bathing revolution in the late 1960s. He felt that a bathroom should be not only functionally efficient (although without a stark hospital appearance), but also as attractive, soothing and invigorating as any other room, with character, colour and luxury. The famous Hicksian love of geometric pattern is currently undergoing a revival, albeit without the designer's signature felted walls, masses of cotton curtains, or carpets underfoot. Otherwise, there appears to be another general trend for men to shower and women to bathe. Ideally, however, no house or apartment, no matter how small, should be without both facilities.

Bathing at home has a long and varied history: what seem to be the most contemporary, free-standing oval stone baths hark back to the eighteenth century and beyond; marble finishes are more popular than ever; and Victorian roll-top baths, with their splayed, shell-shaped feet, are found in many town and country bathrooms. Shower cubicles have grown in size, and are often specially plumbed to create power showers, producing steaming downpours from enormous ceiling-mounted chrome fittings. Along with 'wet rooms', the delivery of great volumes of water represents the greatest change in bathroom design. As a result, heated towel rails, once a novelty, are essential, while every bathing-space should ideally have underfloor heating. Perhaps not quite as subject to fashion diktats as the kitchen – which, as we have seen, is now an important living-space – the bathroom is a more private, indeed contemplative affair, and if the initial outlay is invested in its design and quality materials and fittings, the finished room can, and should, have a long life.

Contemporary

More than applies to any other room, the design of a bathroom is dictated by (often too little) space and plumbing possibilities. Nonetheless, as families shrink in size and more people choose to live alone, former bedrooms are frequently being converted into luxurious multi-purpose bathing, showering and storage spaces, no longer simply or primarily utilitarian but treated to fine finishes where the emphasis is not only on function but also on beauty. 'Spa-bathing' is the modern buzz word: ideas taken from the great spa hotels and resorts are translated and given a domestic twist. Obviously, everything has to be scaled down, but the essential elements of luxury, light, relaxation and pampering remain key. While contemporary bathrooms lack traditional decoration, other qualities – apart from just plenty of space – are valued: perfectly lit mirrors, plenty of warm towels and, despite the environmental issues at stake, limitless hot water.

Contemporary

Contemporary bathroom design rarely favours the pedestal washbasin. Instead, basins made of glass, stainless steel or porcelain are top-mounted (where the basin is set on top of the surface, like a bowl) or set flush into whatever vanity surface is chosen – and the choice is wide. Stone, marble, glossy timber, polished concrete: almost anything goes.

How often does the seasoned and tired traveller lament hotel or bed-and-breakfast bathroom designs, where there is nowhere to put a toothbrush or cosmetics, apart from, perhaps, a too-narrow shelf above the basin, or – in the last resort – on the floor. Excellent use of space is illustrated here (left and below, left), where in each case the basin fills the width of a niche, providing plenty of usable surface area. Wall-mounted taps keep the wet area free of clutter. The charcoal *tadelakt* guest bathroom in a Moroccan house (opposite) might be gloomy in a London home, but a wall of glass giving on to a tiny courtyard is not only contemporary but also exotic (albeit dependent on enjoying a private location).

Traditional

Four of the bathrooms illustrated here
are in French country houses; the fifth
is in an old house in central Antwerp
(opposite, top right). In each case, they
have been treated to more decorative,
soft and tactile elements than are found in
the truly contemporary bathroom. They
are furnished rather than fitted, and also
spacious and perfectly in keeping with
the architecture of each of the buildings.
Antique mirrors and light-fittings add
glamour. For each bathroom the owners
have chosen side-mounted taps and
a hand-held shower-fitting to enable
comfortable reclining in a deep, broad,
old-fashioned bath. Old wooden
floorboards have been retained; when
waxed and waterproofed, they are almost
as good as any other surface, although
perhaps less suitable for exuberant
children. Nostalgia is part of this style's
enduring appeal.

Traditional

Here, in an Irish castle (above), a large former bedroom has been used to create a wonderful bathroom. The window is Georgian, the bath placed opposite to provide an unrivalled view. The bath panels, painted a soft grey-lilac, echo, and are in keeping with, the full-height wall panelling. A chandelier and antique furniture complete the sense of country-house splendour.

A gleaming white roll-top bath was chosen for a modern South African home in the bush (above, right), as well as for a French country house (opposite, left). Both baths look appropriate, despite their very different settings. The painted panelling, pretty shelves and sash window looking on to a garden (opposite, right) would seem to suggest a house in the English countryside, but in fact this elegant bathroom is in London. Where a bath is placed against a wall,

as here, a surround of hardwood, stone or marble is a practical and perennially popular way to provide a neat finish.

Traditional

Guest cloakrooms have long been treated as print rooms, a place to display amusing political cartoons or – in Britain at least – illustrations of country pursuits. This is part of a tradition in which the cloakroom or bathroom is decorated, enhanced and treated in a less utilitarian fashion and more as part of the integral style of an entire house. It does not mean that practicalities and function are ignored, but the choice, as we have seen earlier (pages 270–71), of mirrors, lighting and furniture, together with pictures, creates a period ambience. Where the bathroom is en-suite to a bedroom, carpet may be used on the floor, although this can be difficult to keep dry if the bathroom is in constant use. Chairs, window seats or stools will often have towelling covers, and extra-large bath mats may be provided. For some, the effect is too cosy, too country and impractical, but there is nonetheless something undeniably romantic and inviting about a bathroom treated as a comfortable living-space.

Natural Materials

So large is the circular shower in an ancient French tower (below, right) that the stone walls were just repointed and left as they were – not a treatment that would suit a smaller space.

Wood, especially modern treated veneers, is popular in bathrooms, where too many hard surfaces can look clinical. In another, equally ancient French chateau (opposite, right), oak wall cladding was extensively used to create a suitably rustic yet elegant finish in various rooms, including a guest cloakroom and the centrally placed master bathroom. The sliding oak door is a neat solution; a panelled door would have appeared unwieldy.

In a London bathroom (below, left), the old wooden strip floor was retained; this, with the choice of an antique, beautifully figured dressing commode, adds to the sense of stepping into the residence of a nineteenth-century gentleman.

Patterned Surfaces

Although some people opt for a plain, neutral and quiet bathroom scheme, in which the bather can unwind in total and undistracted tranquillity, there is also a case for using vibrant decorative styles in the bathroom, where they can be appreciated at leisure. Four very different ways of using pattern in bathrooms are illustrated here, the most exuberant and original being the tulip design painted directly on to the wall of a bathroom in Antwerp by the room's owner, an artist, garden designer and tulip expert. For a guest bathroom in a Thames-side apartment (opposite, left), a London designer opted for sheer luxury, and chose a hand-leafed, white-gold paper from de Gournay for the walls, and Bisazza mosaic tiles for the floor. Both here and in the bathroom shown opposite, right, polished cast-aluminium baths make a statement, one dramatically reflecting the mosaic floor, the other offsetting a wall beautifully painted in 'Pompeiian' style.

In a house in Germany, a vigorous colour scheme of purple and yellow could be described as 'royal regency' (below), pulled together with glossy black paintwork and a gilt-framed mirror.

Textured and Coloured Surfaces

Rather than using tiles or stone on the walls, the designers of these bathrooms have, in all but one case, looked to other traditional materials. The charcoal *tadelakt* (opposite, top) is almost iridescent in natural light. Easy to apply, it has been used on every surface, including the sunken bath. It is equally easy to colour with various pigments: the same finish in a soft apricot-ochre tone combines well with the handmade brass basin and taps in a house in Marrakesh (opposite, bottom left).

Earth colours are calm and unobtrusive, and where there is plenty of wall space and towering ceilings (above, left), it makes sense to treat the entire en-suite space to a matt, textured-plaster finish, a little like a traditional African mud building. In such a large space, waterproofing is less important, especially where the bath is free-standing in the centre of the room.

Marble and Stone Surfaces

From entire walls and vanity units lined with expensive book-matched marble slabs, as seen here in a villa on the Spanish coast (right), to a simple, understated, slim grey marble strip along the side of a bath (opposite, bottom left), marble and stone in numerous colours and patterns are the most interesting, hard-wearing and manageable materials for wet areas. Since they are available in very large pieces, and therefore require the minimum of joints and grouting, these materials produce an effect that is far more architectural and solid than tiling. Purists would choose a single material, but here there is a mix, showing the many possibilities on offer.

A stone-lined shower with a softer, slatted timber floor (opposite, bottom right) helps to create a smart but nonetheless inviting room. In a more uncompromising effect, pale creamy stone basins and an extended splashback look sharp and chic against walls clad with horizontal textured tiles (opposite, top).

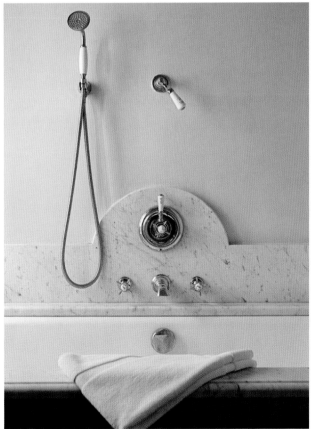

Tiled Surfaces

Whether plain or patterned mosaic, pearl-glazed or with a honed finish, tiling is versatile, hard-wearing, relatively easy to clean, and provides endless creative possibilities. Tiny pale-green tiles have been used for the floor and walls of a London wet room (opposite, left), which appears modern, but simultaneously exudes a period atmosphere of great simplicity, thanks to the exposed pipework of the shower fitting and the large basin. Stone or ceramic tiling may be used in a multitude of ways; as shown here, the completed effect will differ depending on the size and shape of each tile and the colour chosen for the grouting. This bath (above), in a Moroccan riad, is lined with handmade tiles, which are anything but uniform. The subtle tones of the polished-plaster walls suit the artisan look of the tiling, in a style that contrasts completely with the strict lines imposed in the shower in a Sussex house (opposite, right).

Floor Tiles

As is the case with wall and countertop tiles (see pages 144–45), floor tiles can be any shape, size or colour, and ceramic, slate or clay, glossy or matt, patterned or plain. Except where an owner or designer is looking for a seamless, box-like effect, the same tiles are not usually chosen for both the floor and the walls, however. In an ancient French chateau (opposite, left), the owner has restored or replaced the original hexagonal, handmade tiles, their subtle variations in colour appearing rustic, their unglazed surface soft underfoot. A black-and-white chequerboard composition, more often seen in entrance halls, works well in a bathroom hung with a collection of grand portrait prints (far left).

The choice of floor tile, as with wall tiles selected for kitchens, is often made according to local tradition, with various forms of terracotta being the most common. Tile-making has become highly sophisticated, and tiles can now be found, or specially commissioned, that successfully imitate almost every possible type of surface.

Showers

From a mere hole in the wall to an entire wet room, a shower can be created in virtually any location that has plumbing and – critically – drainage. The creativity displayed in the design of showers is boundless. From the curved and tiled enclosure built beneath stairs to a basement playroom (above, left), to the treatment of another basement, this time vaulted with lighting designed to imitate the night sky (right), many are both practical and lovely to look at. Most showerheads are wall-mounted and detachable, although a combination of a fixed overhead spray with a movable one has become de rigueur. Glass screens are popular, but, where space and lifestyle allow, no screen at all is ideal. Wall niches in a Moroccan top-lit shower room (opposite, left) make a good alternative to shelves, keeping the finish smooth and of a single material.

Taps

Modern taps are quite different from their old-fashioned, often brass and now unpopular, counterparts, but old-style chrome or nickel taps in a new bathroom or, conversely, new taps in an old-style bathroom can work equally well. The simplified swan-necked shapes of the single mixer taps seen here (opposite, top and bottom left) have a history that goes back to the eighteenth century, when finely crafted, lifelike bronze or brass swan's-head fittings came into fashion. Surprisingly, a gold-plated version, although rather unfashionable nowadays, was considered the height of luxury until not so long ago. As we have seen already in the kitchen, fittings have become sculptural in an entirely modern way – spare and simple, with the single mixer tap much favoured over the inconvenience of a supply of only hot or cold water. If the devil is in the detail, taps can be said as never before to make an undoubted statement about one's style.

Simple Mirrors

Mirror glass is one of the most useful and exciting materials known to man. Apart from reflecting a perfect image, most often required in a bathroom, it enhances, expands and lights the space in which it is hung – or propped, or balanced, or fixed to a wall. Where baths or basins are set into a niche or a recess, a large mirror will prevent any feeling of being boxed in, particularly where the mirror is set away from the wall and backlit. This English country house (opposite, right) offers a wonderful solution to the old problem of how to provide good-sized mirrors when washbasins are set under windows. The mirrors are fixed to the basins and lined up with the taps, so there is still plenty of room to open the windows and use the linen blind behind. This is a fine example of thoughtful modern design.

Miscellaneous Mirrors

Mirrored furniture, popular in the 1930s, has made a great comeback. Designed like a piece of free-standing furniture, a mirror-clad vanity unit (right) adds femininity and a touch of whimsy to a rigorously designed bathing-space. The tailored blind above perfectly balances the shape of the doors below. Similarly, when choosing mirrors for two bathrooms in a Provençal manor house, the owner has taken the oval shape of a traditional window as the inspiration for pairs of mirrors (below, left and right).

Floor-to-ceiling mirror panels (opposite, right), chosen by a London interior designer for his own home, do a magnificent job of enhancing and expanding the space. Extra-wide washbasins mounted on a 'floating' surface in another London bathroom (opposite, left) called for an equally strong solution involving the use of mirror panels. The black frame of mirror upon mirror creates an interesting link to the shape of the basins, and echoes the black surface of the countertop.

Outdoor Spaces

There is a freedom about being able to step outside or, indeed, look out on a private space; the informality and the sense of getting away from it all are palpable. Outdoor or 'breathing' space – from a humble balcony to a shady town garden, a basement patio to a sweeping country landscape, and from a coastal terrace to a Moroccan courtyard – has become so coveted and valuable that the effort, expense, design and furnishing of the smallest garden 'room' are taken more seriously than ever. Landscape designers and gardeners used to bemoan the fact that clients allocated larger budgets to architects for building or restoration; now the reverse is becoming more common.

The indoor–outdoor links between a house and its garden, terrace or swimming pool are factored into the overall design at an early stage. Other key elements are easy access, a minimum change of materials, the availability of both sunlight and shade, and, above all, our enduring, undiminished love and need for plants. If a theme emerges from the following images, it is one of modernity: urban fashion dictates a pared-down, spare style that is low maintenance, disciplined and angular. The background planting tends to be principally green on green against white walls, limestone terraces and paths; casual cotton or linen upholstery is chosen for the furniture; and the overriding aim is to create a sense of relaxation and calm.

In the country, outdoor living still relies on hard landscaping to link house and garden, where sheltered seating areas are prized year-round. And whether the space is covered or not, and whether one is on holiday or at home, the opportunity to spend time outside in a tranquil place is the aspiration of many.

Lounging
Garden

Lounging is about doing nothing in comfort. For a garden or terrace, the choice of furniture – from simple old-fashioned deckchairs to modern moulded plastic – is all about just that, as well as practicality; standing up to the weather or being easy to store away.

Lounging is a low-level activity, an opportunity to sunbathe, sleep or just daydream. The best outdoor lounging-area ideally provides a lovely view – not usually possible in city gardens, where the focus is centred on a table or perhaps a water feature or sculpture. Brick or stucco walls often form the boundaries, providing enclosure and retaining warmth. In narrow suburban gardens (opposite, bottom), hedges make a softer boundary and eliminate the need for much additional planting; here, the seating area is delineated by paving giving on to cool grass.

Lounging
Patio, Deck and Roof

The creation of a surface for outdoor living depends very much on the surroundings and architecture involved. Teak or other hardwood decking has become very popular both in town and in the country: it is easy to lay, cool underfoot and needs little maintenance, the colour soon fading to soft-grey hues. Such a surface can appear rustic or sophisticated, depending on how and where it is placed.

Creamy slabs of stone are a more appropriate material for the penthouse of an iconic twentieth-century apartment building in north London, which has balconies and seating spaces connected to virtually every room. Meanwhile, in Spain (opposite, bottom), the stone flooring echoes the 'blockiness' of the design and the careful layout of the cushions. The look is streamlined and tailored, yet such seating, built up against a courtyard wall, provides copious and comfortable space in which to stretch out with a newspaper or book.

Lounging
Seaside

There is nothing quite as relaxing as being at the seaside. Whether one is simply splayed on a towel on the beach; leaning into soft pillows on oak-framed sofas the colour of driftwood, set on a terrace high above a cliff; or whiling away the hours on a Tuscan-style porch framed with breezy muslin curtains, the whole point of seaside living is to enjoy the view. Ever-changing cloud formations, the backwash of the ocean, and the feeling of being in touch with nature provide a constant source of peaceful entertainment and pleasure, as one's mind drifts and centres somewhere in the distance across an expanse of sea. To ensure real comfort, daybeds are preferable to conventional chairs.

For seaside outdoor spaces, softer, neutral colours, enhanced by striped fabrics or pure-white canvas, work well. The exterior of the house is best kept simple: painted clapboard, stone or white stucco are all effective and relatively easy to maintain against the weathering sea air.

Lounging
Under Cover

Covered terraces take many forms. In Provence, beamed and tiled roofs create useful extensions to a house during both hot summers and rainy spells. Sometimes just partly covered, the enclosed area can be treated much more like an indoor room; below, a large mirror is well placed to reflect light and to create a sense of a much larger space.

The ultimate luxury, however, must be bedrooms where the glass walls 'disappear'. Given that there are no neighbours, one can sleep in the semi-open air, as illustrated here (left) in the South African bush. The space is designed to allow the owners to move easily from sleep to a sunny terrace and thence into a swimming pool; the surfaces are all on one level. Daybeds and loungers are strategically placed at various points to capture the shade and to allow the occupants to take in at leisure the extraordinary views.

Dining Outside
Contemporary Covered

The way in which a modern terrace is covered, or protected as a dining-space, often involves the use of local or traditional materials. At a Modernist new house outside Marrakesh (opposite, bottom), a roof of eucalyptus poles filters and softens the unrelenting summer sunlight above the seating- and dining-areas. A dining-terrace at a house above the town of Lucca in Italy (below) uses cane matting simply attached to slim metal poles, in a solution that is both cheap and effective. Quite different is the extended roof of a Huf house in Germany (opposite, top right), dating from the 1980s; the roof-line is original, but the paving and level garden were reworked in a more contemporary manner. In a similar vein, but more reminiscent of the Palm Springs style of the 1950s, the architect of a new house in the southern French region of the Var angled the single column support to a curving roof-line (right). In preparation for both summer and winter dining, a terrace in southern Spain (opposite, top left) has not only a practical, tile-topped table, but also an iroko timber screen that can be covered by electronically operated blinds.

Dining Outside
Traditional Covered

In much of northern Europe and parts of the United States, dining out of doors is a hit-and-miss activity. The 'winter garden' evolved in the nineteenth century to provide a partly glazed, south-facing room in which one could spend time during the cooler months and grow tender flowering plants. From horticultural glasshouses developed the conservatory, a protected, attached living-space, heated and treated as part of the house.

As few people enjoy dining in direct sunlight, in hotter climates, permanently covered terraces are important living- and dining-rooms, set up formally or informally, and often sited – naturally – to maximize a view. The owner of a village house in the South of France (opposite, right) spends a great deal of time on her first-floor terrace. Full of shrubs, flowers and climbers, the space imitates a proper garden, with areas of light and shadow.

Furniture for these outdoor spaces tends to be more relaxed than that found in indoor dining-rooms. The large orangery-style conservatory overlooking an English country garden (right) shows an old-fashioned kitchen table teamed with *Victoria Ghost* chairs and a wonderfully decorative chandelier. In such an effortlessly grand setting, there is no need for upholstery, tablecloths or the other trappings of formal dining.

Dining Outside
Contemporary Open-Air

Whether upon urban rooftops or in country gardens, spaces allocated for open-air dining can be any size or shape, but they generally rely on attractive planting to soften the edges, create a sense of enclosure and provide privacy or perspective. In hot climates, dining outside is usually confined to breakfast and dinner, the cooler times of the day that require no

shade. In such cities as London, as long as it is not raining, the outdoor dining experience is greatly valued – witnessed by the burgeoning number of street cafes, their tables set outside even in winter. Above, left, and opposite, bottom left, are two London rooftop terraces. Both are screened by plants; in the one shown opposite, where the view is not entirely enticing, the owner has also fixed several painted metal panels along the railings to enclose the space effectively without creating any sense of it being a courtyard.

The sunny terraces surrounding a chateau in Bordeaux (above, right) have no need of privacy, so the planting is kept low. In southern Italy (opposite, top left), a tiny, imaginatively planted garden wraps around the kitchen terrace on two levels.

For outdoor dining to succeed, the key is always an easy connection to the house or kitchen. Dining without cover is a different experience: lighter, airier and with a greater sense of connection to the great outdoors; a clear sky is canopy enough.

Dining Outside
Traditional Open-Air

A wall of Pierre de Ronsard roses in full bloom and scent – a glorious backdrop to linen-covered chairs and a teak dining-table – can only mean summer in Provence. White slip-covered chairs suggest that the place enjoys regular dry summers and that there is plenty of storage space for the furniture when it is not in use.

There is a traditional feel to these spaces, which feature classic cafe tables and chairs, or various wooden chairs, either painted or oiled. Where white linen tablecloths are used, the scene is redolent of holidays and nostalgia, evoking the promise of long family lunches.

Apart from the view of a long shady terrace stretching the full width of a shuttered Provençal bastide (opposite, top right), these images show areas where dining-tables can be easily moved from one place to another – an important factor. So much about outdoor dining depends on the time of year, so a flexible arrangement that allows one to have breakfast in the early-morning sun or dinner in evening shadow is ideal.

Quiet Courtyards

Houses built around courtyards have ancient historical roots, based on the need for defence and privacy. Most famous today are the riads of old Moroccan towns and cities. Spain, too, through eight hundred years of Moorish influence, adopted this style of building, where warrens of narrow alleyways show faces blind but for, here and there, a single door. Within a riad, a further corridor or several halls ensure that the visitor is slowly introduced into the family living-spaces ranged around the courtyard, which usually sports a small fountain at its centre.

Planting plays an important part in how the space is used. Pots containing olives, oranges or figs – the climate of course allows such planting to thrive – and flowerbeds where hibiscus and bougainvillaea reach for the sky, add an exotic quality.

Quiet Courtyards

The creation of a courtyard often provides an architectural solution to gaining living-space. By excavating a level, walled space on a sloping site in the South of France, the English architect who designed the house below provided not only outdoor seating but also, critically, a double aspect, allowing light into the house at the front and rear.

By their very nature, courtyards, especially when partly covered, tend to be quiet, protected and cosseting spaces. Even here (opposite, right), where the area principally consists simply of old stone steps as an access-way to an upper level, rather than being a real living-space, the addition of flowerpots brimming with pink flowers creates a sense of warm enclosure that is both welcoming and intimate.

Exotic Courtyards

Four of the wholly or partly enclosed areas seen here are in Morocco, while the pink-and-orange cloister walkway within a courtyard is the entrance to a three-sided open area facing the sea in a house in southern Spain. Traditionally, a courtyard would be walled on three or four sides, but the same effect can be gained by a single high wall or – as seen here in a villa designed by Jean-François Zevaco – an exotic, partly enclosed living-area, created by adding an open timber roof.

Rooftops are not normally associated with courtyards, but in Marrakesh (right), where women traditionally used the flat rooftops as secluded areas in which to congregate, a rooftop with raised walls provides intimacy and privacy. In the same riad the ground level (below) is darker, much cooler and more mysterious.

Large Pools

Indoors or out, large swimming pools can both satisfy an owner's desire for a perfect form of exercise – swimmers, like runners, can become obsessive – and, when set in a garden and designed to be more like a lake or pond, provide a facility around which, in the heat of the summer, one can simply relax and cool off.

A large infinity pool, seen here (opposite, top) raised above the level of a house in Provence, is a spectacular addition to the sloping site. Water slides over the front edge of the stone retaining wall, creating a mirror-like effect from the terraces below. In Marrakesh (above, right), an enormous pool, complete with tiled islands and palm trees, fills the space in front of the house.

Water, with its complex and dazzling reflective potential, often stimulates designers to create sensational visions. By lining up a rill directly on the central glass wall of an extraordinary indoor pool in southern England (opposite, bottom), the architect has achieved the ultimate sense of connection to the landscape, while ensuring that swimming can be a year-round activity. The dramatic approach to this Spanish pool (above, left) between a pair of tile-roofed pavilions reveals a spectacular, hilly setting where the end of the pool is perched above a sheer drop.

Poolside Loungers and Umbrellas

The choice of poolside furniture varies greatly, but such furnishings need to meet the two criteria for relaxing outdoors: comfort and shade. White canvas umbrellas have become state-of-the-art design pieces, able to withstand high winds or rain, and are being designed larger than ever. In complete contrast, in this home in the African bush (opposite, top right), a simple woven, conical shade looks perfect teamed with a basket-like seat.

Hardwearing timber or lightweight man-made fibre loungers are usually adjustable, allowing the user either to sit up or to lie flat, as if on a bed, in the sun or shade. While seating is often laid out in pairs, to encourage people to be sociable, or – at the beginning of the day – in south-facing lines, serious sun-worshippers will move themselves around as the day wears on, positioning themselves for the best angle and, perhaps, the best view.

Small Pools and Water Features

The sight and sound of water do much to calm and cool our senses, especially in hot climates. Traditional Moroccan courtyards always include a fountain or larger water feature. In the transitional space between a Moroccan house and its salon (opposite, top left), the architect placed a low, flower-like marble basin in the centre of a reflecting pool.

In Provence, another courtyard house, created from a group of old warehouses, has a raised concrete pool with a Classical-shaped water-spout against a wall. The pool provides enough room to cool off, but with a nod to a classic French *bassin*. A series of curved, different-sized pools in a South African game lodge (opposite, bottom left) cleverly imitates the flow of a river beside the decked terraces.

House Index

This index gives information about the design and architecture of the 100 houses featured in the book. Houses are numbered according to the order in which they first appear. Page references below each image in the index show where the larger-scale image appears in the book.

1

Architecture/restoration/design: Claire Perraton, c/o Bureau d'Études Bruno & Alexandre Lafourcade, 10 Boulevard Victor Hugo, BP 75, 13532 St-Rémy-de-Provence, France; +33 (0)4 90 92 10 14; architecture-lafourcade.com.

Garden design: Dominique Lafourcade.

Page 2

Page 34

Page 107

Page 158

Page 188

Page 232

Page 242

Page 246

Page 273

Page 294

Page 294

2

Design: Edric van Vredenburgh; vanvredenburgh.com.

Art: p. 253, bottom right: painting by window by François Arnal.

Page 7

Page 227

Page 253

Page 276

3

Architecture: Michael Edwards. Design: John Minshaw, 17 Upper Wimpole Street, London W1G 6LU; +44 (0)20 7486 5777; johnminshawdesigns.com.

Art: p. 83, left: torso sculpture by Emily Young; p. 192, top: painting by Edward Povey.

Page 8

Page 21

Page 33

Page 42

Page 62

Page 80

Page 80

Page 83

Page 94

Page 128

Page 148

Page 152

Page 178

Page 192

Page 193

Page 212

Page 220

Page 253

Page 271

Page 288

Page 292

Page 320

4

Design: Carrie Belotti and Cheryl Tague; cheryltague.com.

Art: p. 28, top right: painting by Chris Cox.

Page 11

Page 28

Page 53

Page 180

Page 209

5

Architecture: Project Orange. Design: Isas Sastraada, Sastraada Design Ltd, 821 Fulham Road, London SW6 5HG; +44 (0)20 7998 1908; sastraadadesign.com.

Art: p. 17 and p. 42, top: work above fireplace by Steve Smulka.

Pages 12, 17

Page 42

Page 54

Page 56

Page 61

Page 119

Page 226

Page 267

Page 267

Page 291

6

Architecture: Hut Architects; hutarchitecture.com.

Decoration: John Carver and Anna Carver; cunning.com.

Kitchen design: Neil Jolliffe.

Page 14

Page 62

Page 146

Page 249

Page 284

7

Property development/design: Candy & Candy; candyandcandy.com.

Page 15

Page 30

Page 50

Page 87

Page 120

Page 164

Page 165

Page 211

Page 251

Page 268

Page 299

8

Architecture/restoration/design: Smiros & Smiros; +1 516 676 9200; smiros.com.

Page 15

Page 106

Page 150

Page 184

Page 238

Page 286

Page 287

9

Architecture: Alfredas Trimonis, Hackel-Kaape Trimonis Architekten, Sierichstrasse 38D, 22301 Hamburg, Germany; h-k-t-hamburg.de.

Page 16

Page 61

Page 71

Page 80

Page 203

Page 251

10

Original architecture/design: Bertold Lubetkin.

Contemporary design/decoration: Ou Baholyodhin; ou-b.com.

Page 16

Page 46

Page 48

Page 48

Page 82

Page 202

Page 210

Page 301

11

Design: Doug Atherley BIDA, IIDA, Kinari Design Limited, 29 Clarendon Road, London W11 4JB; +44 (0)20 7221 9569; kinaridesign.com.

Art: p. 16, top left: picture above Chinese chair, *Fall* by Bridget Leaman; mirror above fireplace by Eduardo Samso; p. 53, left: yellow mixed-media painting above fireplace, *Untitled* by Andrew Johnstone; p. 110, top: stainless-steel sculpture, *Leaping Cat* by Clare Biggar; p. 164, top left: photograph to right of blue flowers, *Blue ice and oak leaves* by John Wawrzonek.

Page 16

Page 53

Page 66

Page 110

Page 164

Page 236

Page 257

Page 268

Page 298

12

Interior design: Louise Jones Interiors, Fairbanks Studios 2, 65–69 Lots Road, London SW10 0RN; +44 (0)20 7351 6858; louisejonesinteriors.com.

Art: p. 230: painting above commode, *Balenciaga Dress* by Richard Nott.

Page 16

Page 32

Page 63

Page 64

Page 87

Page 89

Page 103

Page 104

Page 105

Page 108

Page 122

Page 137

Page 141

Page 142

Page 170

Page 185

Page 208

Page 226

Page 230

Page 235

Page 254

Page 266

Page 266

Page 268

Page 277

Page 283

Page 291

Page 292

Page 294

13

Architecture/design: Pasquale Amodio and Randa Hanna, Map Projects Ltd, 60 Southwark Bridge Road, London SE1 0AS; +44 (0)20 7633 9955; mapprojects.com.

Art: p. 208, bottom left: silk-screen map of the world by Kee Levi.

Page 18

Page 61

Page 76

Page 120

Page 140

Page 155

Page 192

Page 208

14

Design: Fernando Carrizosa-Kolbe, Marbella/Puerto Banus; interiorissimofck.com.

Art: p. 95: painting of woman by Santiago Carbonell; p. 185, left: painting by Santiago Carbonell.

Page 18

Page 40

Page 95

Page 185

Page 234

Page 282

Page 283

Page 303

Page 323

15

Architecture: Jean-François Zevaco.

Art: p. 19, top: painting by Mohamed Bennani; seven pieces of oak furniture/sculpture by Olivier Serguin; p. 69, top right: oak furniture/sculpture by Olivier Serguin.

Page 19

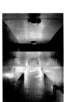
Page 68

Page 69

Page 91

Page 167

Page 318

Page 321

Page 324

16

Design/decoration: Gareth Smith, 8 The Lightworks, 31 Blenheim Gardens, London SW2 5EU; +44 (0)20 8678 7767; Garethdevonaldsmith@gmail.com; commissionacraftsman.com.

Page 19

Page 28

Page 156

Page 311

17

Design: Tanguy Rolin, Tanguy Rolin Ltd, Arch 8,
Crucifix Lane, London SE1 3JW; +44 (0)20 7357 0772;
tanguyrolin.co.uk.

Art: p. 19, centre: painting by Jordi Labanda.

Page 19

Page 26

Page 41

Page 61

Page 89

Page 103

Page 132

Page 257

Page 257

18

Architecture/restoration/design: Bureau d'Études
Bruno & Alexandre Lafourcade, 10 Boulevard Victor Hugo,
BP 75, 13532 St-Rémy-de-Provence, France;
+33 (0)4 90 92 10 14; architecture-lafourcade.com.

Garden design: Dominique Lafourcade.

Page 19

Page 81

Page 210

Page 252

Page 255

Page 262

Page 302

Page 322

19

Architecture/restoration: Studio Barsotti-Giammattei,
Lucca.

Design: Claire and Tom Lester.

Page 20

Page 161

Page 221

Page 231

Page 307

Page 322

Page 323

20

Design: Rui Ribeiro, Rui Ribeiro Interiors;
+44 (0)7717 055 442; rribeiro@msn.com.

Page 20

Page 33

Page 263

Page 293

21

Design: Dorothee von Rheinbaben.

Page 21

Page 59

Page 79

Page 114

Page 114

Page 137

Page 181

Page 188

Page 204

Page 243

Page 244

Page 245

Page 286

22

Design: Kate Earle, Todhunter Earle Interiors, Chelsea Reach, 1st Floor, 79–89 Lots Road, London SW10 0RN; +44 (0)20 7349 9999; todhunterearle.com.

Page 22

Page 33

Page 99

Page 136

Page 149

Page 172

Page 237

Page 237

Page 243

Page 260

Page 272

Page 275

23

Decoration: Natalie Vilmorin.

Page 22

Page 29

Page 46

Page 113

Page 130

Page 160

Page 202

Page 239

24

Design: Kate Earle, Todhunter Earle Interiors, Chelsea Reach, 1st Floor, 79–89 Lots Road, London SW10 0RN; +44 (0)20 7349 9999; todhunterearle.com.

Page 23

Page 45

Page 93

Page 101

Page 110

Page 127

Page 173

Page 188

Page 220

Page 241

Page 260

Page 262

25

Decoration: Christopher Vane Percy, CVP Designs Ltd,
The Old Dairy, 7 Hewer Street, London W10 6DU;
+44 (0)20 8960 9026; cvpdesigns.com.

Page 23

Page 34

Page 38

Page 99

Page 134

Page 181

Page 223

26

Design: Peter Nolden, Peter Interiors, Isestrasse 84,
20149 Hamburg, Germany; +49 (0)40 48 25 09;
peter-interior.de.

Page 23

Page 38

Page 72

Page 76

Page 77

Page 129

Page 162

Page 205

Page 246

27

Decoration: Gerd and Christine Sander.

Page 23

Page 82

Page 92

Page 108

Page 271

Page 271

28

Design: Sebastian Conran, Studio Conran, 22 Shad
Thames, London SE1 2YU; +44 (0)20 7827 4355;
studioconran.com.

Art: p. 24, top left: three works on right by Ian Darrah.

Page 24

Page 107

Page 120

Page 171

Page 195

29

Design: Mark Hix and Clare Lattin.

Page 24

Page 124

Page 134

Page 145

Page 202

Page 228

Page 284

30

Architecture/design: Alexandre Lafourcade, Bureau d'Études Bruno & Alexandre Lafourcade, 10 Boulevard Victor Hugo, BP 75, 13532 St-Rémy-de-Provence, France; +33 (0)4 90 92 10 14; architecture-lafourcade.com.

Garden design: Dominique Lafourcade.

Page 24

Page 24

Page 75

Page 100

Page 115

Page 115

Page 148

Page 151

Page 157

Page 164

Page 300

Page 311

Page 324

31

Architecture: Olivier Moureau and Anthony Julen.

Design: Romain Michel-Meniere, romainmichelmeniere@me.com.

Page 25

Page 86

Page 91

Page 98

Page 109

Page 182

Page 213

Page 225

Page 269

Page 280

Page 281

Page 306

Page 318

32

Design: Anna Bennett; atnbennett@analyzeart.com; analyzeart.com.

Art: p. 25: textile on wall by Annie Sherburne; p. 170, bottom: painting by Zeiya Vandenburg; p. 204, bottom right: animal-sculpture book markers by Berend Hoekstra.

Page 25

Page 55

Page 110

Page 170

Page 204

Page 205

Page 211

33

Architecture: François Narbonne.

Design: Kate Earle, Todhunter Earle Interiors, Chelsea Reach, 1st Floor, 79–89 Lots Road, London SW10 0RN; +44 (0)20 7349 9999; todhunterearle.com.

Art: p. 26, top left and bottom: painting on oak wall by Onyx de Vritz; p. 277, far right: collage, *Coral Wall* by Jacques Barbier.

Page 26

Page 26

Page 57

Page 65

Page 76

Page 116

Page 151

Page 183

Page 217

Page 256

Page 258

Page 277

Page 277

Page 298

Page 27

Page 50

Page 144

Page 200

Page 208

Page 268

34

Architecture/design: Matteo Thun & Partners; matteothun.com.

Page 306

35

Design/decoration: Tomasz Starzewski and Tessa Kennedy, starzewski.com; tessakennedydesign.com.

Art: p. 28, bottom right: portrait by Emma Sargent.

Page 28

Page 90

Page 240

Page 242

36

Design: Emily Todhunter, Todhunter Earle Interiors, Chelsea Reach, 1st Floor, 79–89 Lots Road, London SW10 0RN; +44 (0)20 7349 9999; todhunterearle.com.

Page 29

Page 119

Page 224

Page 255

37

Design: Susanne Bisovsky and Josef Gerger.

Page 29

Page 126

Page 130

Page 163

Page 230

Page 255

Page 259

38

Design: Jane Churchill Interiors, 81 Pimlico Road, London SW1W 8PH; +44 (0)20 7730 8564; janechurchillinteriors.co.uk.

Art: p. 35, top: painting above sofa by Bianca Smith.

Page 29

Page 35

Page 45

Page 259

Page 274

39

Art: p. 30, left: painting on left, *Snowflake* by M. Dumas; painting in centre, *Bruised* by Paula Rego; painting on right, *Rome* by Gary Hume; p. 49, top right: *Untitled Birthday Card* by Damien Hirst; p. 181, bottom right: *Iris II* by William Kentridge; p. 216, top: *Getting Ready for the Ball* by Paula Rego.

Page 30

Page 49

Page 123

Page 181

Page 216

Page 221

40

Architecture/restoration: Bureau d'Études Bruno & Alexandre Lafourcade, 10 Boulevard Victor Hugo, BP 75, 13532 St-Rémy-de-Provence, France; +33 (0)4 90 92 10 14; architecture-lafourcade.com.

Page 30

Page 69

Page 101

Page 104

Page 144

Page 180

Page 242

Page 305

Page 308

41

Decoration: Yvonne and Peter Moore.

Page 31

Page 47

Page 52

Page 128

Page 134

Page 147

Page 222

Page 243

Page 300

Page 312

Page 316

Page 323

42

Architecture/design: Colin Gold; colingold.design@tiscali.co.uk.

Garden design: Robert O'Dea.

Page 33

Page 142

Page 165

Page 230

Page 230

Page 241

337

43

Design: Ronald van der Hilst, Mechelseplein 21–23, 2000 Antwerp, Belgium; +32 (0)3 213 2478; hilst@pandora.be; ronaldvanderhilst.com.

Art: p. 33, left centre: group of pictures above sofa, *Tulips* by Ronald van der Hilst.

44

Architecture: Carolyn Trevor; tlastudio.co.uk.

Art: p. 58, top: picture on left of fireplace by Teddy Millington Drake.

45

Design/decoration: Linda and Ian Swan.

46

Design/decoration: Gemma and Andrew McAlpine.

Art: p. 35, bottom: large black-and-white work behind lilac chair by Basil Beattie; portrait of woman on left of fireplace by Robin Kawakewa.

47

Design: Grant White, 1 Parsons Green Depot, Parsons Green Lane, London SW6 4HH; +44 (0)20 7736 5858; grantwhitedesign.com.

48

Design: Mathias Schneider, Elbchaussee 394, 22609 Hamburg, Germany; +49 (0)40 44 36 31.

Page 37

Page 37

Page 70

Page 90

Page 176

49

Architecture: Legorreta & Legorreta; lmasl.com.mx; legorretalegorreta.com.

Art: p. 39, top left and p. 155, bottom right: photographs above table by Axel Hütte.

Page 39

Page 84

Page 92

Page 118

Page 140

Page 155

Page 228

Page 282

Page 291

Page 301

Page 318

Page 325

50

Design/decoration: Johanna Thornycroft.

Page 39

Page 69

Page 131

Page 173

51

Design: Emma Abdy-Collins, Little Faringdon House, Little Faringdon, Lechlade, Glos. GL7 3QN; +44 (0)1367 252 155; littlefaringdonhouse.co.uk.

Page 39

Page 54

Page 63

Page 104

Page 106

Page 132

Page 169

Page 177

Page 247

Page 274

Page 275

Page 309

52

Architecture/restoration: Bureau d'Études Bruno & Alexandre Lafourcade, 10 Boulevard Victor Hugo, BP 75, 13532 St-Rémy-de-Provence, France; +33 (0)4 90 92 10 14; architecture-lafourcade.com.

Interior decoration: Françoise Garcin.

Page 39

Page 46

Page 51

Page 124

Page 197

Page 258

Page 292

53

Design: Timothy Everest, Bespoke Tailoring,
32 Elder Street, London E1 6BT, +44 (0)20 7377 5770;
timothyeverest.co.uk.

Page 40

Page 85

Page 113

Page 190

Page 199

54

Design: James Fraser, Avantgardener, 16 Winders Road,
London SW11 3HE; +44 (0)7978 4253;
avantgardener.co.uk.

Art: p. 41, top left: large painting behind sofa on deep-
yellow wall by Biddy Bunzl.

Page 41

Page 94

55

Design/decoration: Graham Viney and Michelle Kay;
grahamvineydesign.co.za.

Architectural adviser: Dan Cruickshank.

Page 41

Page 74

Page 74

Page 86

Page 102

Page 105

Page 111

Page 127

Page 144

Page 175

Page 224

Page 247

Page 288

56

Design: Keech Green Ltd, 414 The Chambers, Chelsea
Harbour Design Centre, London SW10 0XF;
+44 (0)20 7351 5701; keechgreen.com.

Art: p. 42, bottom left: three black-and-white pictures, artist
unknown.

Page 42

Page 140

Page 194

Page 199

Page 213

Page 280

57

Design: Marie-Christine Follenfant.

Page 43

Page 78

Page 96

Page 98

Page 151

Page 198

Page 214

Page 282

Page 285

Page 315

Page 319

Page 319

58

Design: Fiona Adamczewski.

Page 44

Page 112

Page 134

Page 136

Page 261

Page 290

59

Design: Thomas and Lilliana Griem, Target Living; targetliving.com.

Page 44

Page 97

Page 123

Page 178

Page 178

Page 224

Page 257

Page 290

Page 299

60

Design: Mimmi O'Connell, Mimmi O'Connell Design Consultant; +44 (0)20 7752 0474; mimmioconnell.com.

Page 44

Page 180

61

Design: Bart de Beule; arcato.be.

Page 45

Page 54

Page 142

Page 151

Page 174

Page 196

Page 229

Page 254

Page 271

62

Owners/architecture/design/decoration: Kirk Lazarus and Ivor Ichikowitz; molori.co.za.

Page 46

Page 60

Page 87

Page 94

Page 141

Page 167

Page 187

Page 272

Page 281

Page 305

Page 305

Page 323

341

Page 324

63

Design/decoration: Antje Kiewell; +44 (0)20 7371 8245; antje.kiewell@gmail.com.

Page 47 *Page 143* *Page 203* *Page 203* *Page 227* *Page 248*

Page 288

64

Design/decoration: Anna and Aib Barwick; +33 (0)557 40 17 99; chateaurigaud.com.
Chateau available for rent.

Page 47 *Page 82* *Page 108* *Page 128* *Page 225* *Page 228*

Page 247 *Page 271* *Page 276* *Page 287* *Page 310*

65

Art: p. 186: painting, *Spy* by Michael Gillette.

Page 49 *Page 186* *Page 236* *Page 259*

66

Design: David Carter Interior Design, 109 Mile End Road, London E1 4UJ; +44 (0)20 7790 0259 (office); +44 (0)7973 653 944 (mobile); alacarter.com.

Page 49 *Page 52* *Page 52* *Page 71* *Page 99* *Page 159*

Page 162 *Page 196* *Page 205* *Page 244* *Page 263* *Page 279*

67

Design by A.-J. Talbot; a-j@gdfdesigns.com.

Page 50

Page 66

Page 84

Page 137

Page 166

68

Design: Stefanie and Reiner Merkel.

Page 50

Page 81

Page 102

Page 154

Page 179

Page 195

Page 202

Page 239

69

Art: p. 51, right: picture behind chairs by Soledad Sevilla; p. 84, top left: picture on left wall by Joan Hernández Pijuan; picture on right wall by Guillem Nadal; sculpture, *Venus* by William Turnbull; p. 214, top left: photograph of buddha in corridor through guest room by Doug and Mike Starn; top right: painting above bed in main bedroom by Carlos Vergara; on left, photograph on zinc by Pedro Fuentes.

Page 51

Page 70

Page 84

Page 111

Page 143

Page 214

Page 214

Page 250

70

Owners/design: Janet and Barry Stevenson.

Page 54

Page 120

Page 137

Page 155

Page 299

71

Design: Hilary Alexander.

Page 55

Page 59

Page 70

Page 259

Page 311

72

Design: Rose Uniacke, Rose Uniacke Interiors, 76–78 Pimlico Road, London SW1W 8PL; +44 (0)20 7730 7050; roseuniacke.com.

Page 56

Page 108

Page 119

Page 168

Page 199

Page 235

Page 290

73

Architecture/design: Stephen Ryan, Stephen Ryan Design
& Decoration, 7 Clarendon Cross, London W11 4AP;
+44 (0)20 7243 0864; stephenryandesign.com.

Art: p. 57, top: relief work above sofa by Kim James;
p. 189: large painting on wall behind glass table, *Sea Cow*
by Emma Kelly.

Page 57

Page 88

Page 107

Page 143

Page 189

Page 196

Page 225

Page 233

Page 258

Page 290

Page 295

74

Design: Maxine Harrison, MH Design Ltd, Chilmark House,
Chilmark, Salisbury SP3 5AP; +44 (0)7879 625 454;
maxine@mhdesignltd.com.

Page 57

Page 67

Page 149

Page 200

Page 262

75

Design/decoration: Rose Uniacke and Susan Checketts,
Rose Uniacke Interiors, 76–78 Pimlico Road, London
SW1W 8PL; +44 (0)20 7730 7050; roseuniacke.com.

Page 58

Page 138

Page 147

Page 254

76

Design: Bill Bennette ASID, IIDA, FBIID; bbdesign.co.uk.

Page 64

Page 65

Page 74

Page 74

Page 105

Page 178

Page 201

Page 201

Page 252

Page 286

77

Design: Hans-Otto Beute, Poelchaukamp 33, 22301
Hamburg, Germany; +49 40 279 6591.

Art: p. 64: pair of pictures either side of television by
Robert Weber.

Page 64

Page 70

Page 92

Page 225

Page 278

Page 289

78

Design: Penny Morrison, Morrison Interiors, Evancoyd Court, Presteigne, Powys LD8 2PA; +44 (0)1547 560 460; pennymorrison.com.

Page 67

Page 266

Page 302

79

Design/decoration: Donna Ward; donnawdesign@aol.com.

Page 69

Page 126

Page 160

Page 174

Page 188

Page 223

Page 296

Page 309

Page 320

80

lamaisonduvillage.com.

Page 76

Page 231

Page 254

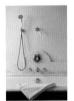
Page 283

81

Architecture/restoration: Bureau d'Études Bruno & Alexandre Lafourcade, 10 Boulevard Victor Hugo, BP 75, 13532 St-Rémy-de-Provence, France; +33 (0)4 90 92 10 14; architecture-lafourcade.com.

Garden design: Dominique Lafourcade.

Interior decoration: Jean-Louis Raynaud and Kenyon Kramer, Antiquités & Decoration, 3 Place des Trois Ormeaux, 13100 Aix-en-Provence, France; +33 (0)4 42 23 52 32.

Page 77

Page 82

Page 103

Page 129

Page 139

Page 180

Page 240

Page 244

Page 294

Page 313

82

Architecture/design/decoration: Kamran Diba; kamrandiba@gmail.com.

Art: p. 78, left: standing figures by Juan Muñoz.

Page 78

Page 321

83

Design: Josee Kayser, +34 (0)607 374 040; reservaslacasa@gmail.com; lacasadesanlucar.com.

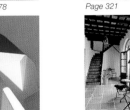
Page 80

Page 83

Page 139

Page 211

Page 219

Page 247

Page 252

Page 286

Page 315

Page 316

84

Owner/design: John Shield.

Page 84

Page 214

Page 218

Page 219

Page 280

Page 289

Page 324

85

Design: David Carter Interior Design, 109 Mile End Road, London E1 4UJ; +44 (0)20 7790 0259 (office); +44 (0)7973 653 944 (mobile); alacarter.com.

Page 86

Page 89

Page 97

Page 212

Page 235

Page 253

Page 264

86

Concept architect: David Price, David Price Design, Les Baux de Provence and Mougins; +33 (0)4 90 54 36 04; +33 (0)4 92 99 15 09; davidpricedesign.com.

Building architect: CASA Architecture Saint Tropez.

Decoration: Cédric Schmitt, La Maison de Cédric, St-Rémy-de-Provence, France.

Page 86

Page 103

Page 121

Page 168

Page 182

Page 226

Page 300

Page 307

Page 317

87

Restoration/design/decoration: Michael and Elisa Catoir, Studio Catoir, Via Vigoni 10, 20122 Milan, Italy; +39 02 3651 6067; studiocatoir.com.

Page 306

Page 88

Page 140

Page 179

Page 228

88

Decoration: Isabelle de Borchgrave; isabelledeborchgrave.com.

Page 99

Page 262

89

Design: Jennifer and Helmut Gorlich, Le Manoir,
34 Rue du Maresquel, 62870 Gouy-St-André,
Pas de Calais, France; +33 (0)3 21 90 47 22.

Page 101

Page 101

Page 114

Page 133

Page 220

Page 237

Page 270

90

Decoration: Gerard Conway; gerard@gerardconway.com.

Page 109

Page 112

Page 189

Page 239

Page 240

91

Design: Colin Gold; colingold.design@tiscali.co.uk.

Art: p. 182, bottom right: glass sculpture by Ioan Nemtoi;
art in frame by Colin Gold.

Page 111

Page 146

Page 182

Page 189

92

Design: Nikki Atkinson, Nikki Atkinson Ltd, Pond House,
Little Coxwell, Oxfordshire SN7 7LW;
UK callers, 07000 10 21 22; international callers
+44 (0) 1367 243530; nikkiatkinson@aolcom.

Page 122

93

Design: John Rendall.

Page 130

Page 326

94

Design: Jo and Madeleine Lee;
swedishinteriordesign.co.uk.

Page 135

Page 147

Page 172

Page 204

Page 217

Page 231

95

Decoration: Katrine Boorman and Danny Moynihan.

Page 136

Page 187

Page 199

Page 216

Page 232

Page 233

Page 235

Page 314

Page 314

96

Design: Mary Gilliatt.

Page 139

Page 258

Page 304

Page 308

97

Design: Anna Maria Quaradeghini, AMQ Interiors, 55 Ebury Street, London SW1W 0PB; +44 (0)20 7730 8008.

Art: p. 154, bottom: work above fireplace by Francesco Patriarca; p. 184, right: video-still above fireplace by Bettina Khano; p. 261, right: picture above dressing-table by Yang Qian.

Page 154

Page 184

Page 261

Page 295

98

Decoration: Jenny Dyer; jennydyerlondon.com.

Page 200

Page 208

Page 298

99

Design/decoration: Rebecca Hill, French Country Living UK Ltd, London and Mougins, France; frenchcountrylivingantiques.com.

Page 234

Page 274

100

Design: Sybil Stanislaus.

Page 310

Page 352

First published 2010 by

Merrell Publishers Limited
81 Southwark Street
London SE1 0HX

merrellpublishers.com

British Library Cataloguing-in-Publication Data:
Einsiedel, Andreas
Dream rooms: inspirational interiors from 100 homes
1. Interior decoration – Pictorial works
I. Title II. Thornycroft, Johanna
747-dc22

ISBN 978-1-8589-4512-5

Produced by Merrell Publishers Limited
Designed by Nicola Bailey
Project-managed by Lucy Smith
Printed and bound in China

Front jacket: house no. 21 (see House Index, p. 332)
Back jacket, top row, left to right: houses nos. 5, 26, 33 and 3 (see pp. 329, 334, 336 and 328); bottom row, left to right: houses nos. 53, 45, 85 and 79 (see pp. 340, 338, 346 and 345)
Frontispiece: house no. 1 (see p. 328)
Introduction images: houses nos. 2, 3 and 4 (see p. 328)
Page 352: house no. 100 (see p. 348)